Moosefart

A man, a woman, and a shattered dream.

Mary Snyder

Steel Roof Press—Ankeny, IA
ISBN: 979-8-9858721-0-1
Library of Congress Control Number: 2022905205
Title: *Moosefart*
Author: Mary Snyder
Digital distribution | 2022
Paperback | 2022

Dedication

For Hoot.
You asked me to tell your story, so here it is.
I hope I have done it justice.

Author's Notes

This is a true story about a real man who I'm calling Steve Hoight. The man is real, but the name is not. My apologies to everyone really named Steve Hoight.

The dialogue in this story is not necessarily the literal words used, but reflect the general conversation whether face to face, through email, or phone calls.

Steve and I knew each other for ten years. Time and details have been condensed for ease of reading.

Acknowledgements

Writing, at least the way I do it, is not done in a vacuum. Thank you to the many people who read the various drafts of this book and gave input to make it stronger, including; Marilyn Snyder, Don Thatcher, Sasha Webster, Jane and Bruce Gandrud, Mark McCurdy, Jaime Rickert, Dr. Mark and Julie Burdt, Bobby Walter, Jane Kennedy, Jackie Tonhouse, Mike Radue, Fr. Bob Aubrey, Fruncle Jim Bruch, Carol and Scott Walters, Cathy and Mike Snyder, Dr. Brooke Oppermann, Kelly Neal, Paul David, Brian Shea, Rachel Corpus, Amy Sun, Phyllis Eddy, Mary Smith, Rose Gilman and many other cheerleaders and general supporters of my writing.

Special thanks to the Costa Rica Omega Institute February 2020 'Writing From the Heart' group led by Nancy Slonim Aronie who enthusiastically supported my writing. Thanks also to Justin Webster and Kim Meller-Angus for graphic help.

Shout outs to the friends and family of Steve Hoight. I won't begin to try and list you all, but you know who you are. Each of us have memories of Steve, and perhaps you will recognize some of the stories in Moosefart.

Table of Contents

Chapter 1
The Beginning

"Why is it so warm in here?" This was my first house. I'd only moved in a few weeks ago and had just walked in the door after working out at the local gym. Were there problems already? The thermostat confirmed that the air conditioning wasn't working. It was July in Iowa and already hot and humid at 8:00 AM.

"That guy I played racquetball doubles with this morning remodels homes," I thought. "Maybe he knows whom I could call. They always call him Hoot, but I don't know his real name." By calling a mutual acquaintance, I learned his real name was Steve Hoight so I grabbed the 1999 Sioux City, Iowa, phone book left by the previous homeowners. I gave him a call, knowing he wouldn't answer because after 3 intense racquetball games Hoot and a few of his gym buddies always cleaned up and went to a local diner for biscuits and gravy. I left a message on his answering machine, showered, and then went to get groceries in air conditioned comfort. I came home to this message.

"Hi Mary, I hear you're the hottest woman in town! Sure, I can take a look at your air conditioner. Give me a call when you're home and I'll come over."

"So how did you get the nickname of Hoot?" I

asked later that day as he was taking tools from his truck backed in my driveway.

"My last name is Hoight and years ago someone pronounced it wrong and said Hoot. It stuck. Some people call me Hooter. A lot of people have no idea my real name is Steve!"

After finishing the repair we waited inside to make sure everything was working and were making idle conversation.

"You have a nice place," he said, looking around. "I bet you and your husband are happy here."

"Thanks," I said, "but no husband."

"Kids?"

"Nope, never married and I have a lot of kids at school but none at home. And this isn't my dream home, but it's a start."

"What's your dream home?"

Most of my family and friends have heard me talk about wanting a log cabin with a steel roof approached by a curved driveway lined with white pines. I told him about it.

He responded with stunned silence. "That's my dream house!" he finally exclaimed.

The house was starting to cool, but it felt like things might be heating up between us.

"I never got as far as the curved driveway and white pines," he admitted, "but I'm wondering what type of wood you plan to use for the house."

"Well, I haven't gotten that far," I admitted. "Do you work in construction?"

"No, I'm self-employed. I own a few apartment buildings and do a lot of handyman work. It lets me write my own schedule and fly or ride or boat whenever I want." He slowly started gathering his tools. "You're a teacher, right?"

"I used to teach music, and I still provide music for weekend church services and give piano lessons, but now I'm a school counselor."

"Oh. Touchy-feely stuff."

"Sometimes," I said, "but it's much more than that. Do you and your wife have kids?"

"No wife, no kids. The only school counselor I knew was the one I had in high school who told me I wasn't college material."

"What did you decide to do after high school?" I asked.

"Went to a community college and learned a trade. Best decision I ever made. I love to figure out how things work." By now we were back at his truck and the tools I saw indicated he made good use of his skills. I didn't mention that the school counselor had probably done him a big favor.

"I can fix some things as a school counselor, but I'm not too mechanical," I said, bringing the conversation back to the original problem. "The reason I called you was to find out who I could trust in town to work on my air conditioner, but I'm glad you were the only call I needed to make. What was the problem?"

"You had a small part that needed to be replaced. It's pretty common, and I had one in my truck," he said.

"Thank you!" I said. "What do I owe you?"

"The part cost about $7.00, but let's forget about that. Why don't you take me out to dinner instead, because I've got something I want to put between your legs."

It was my turn to respond in stunned silence. Dammit! It had been going so well! I was backing away when he winked and said, "I meant my motorcycle!"

In the few days before our dinner, I talked to a racquetball friend about Hoot. She assured me that he was a character but a good kind. I was comfortable on the back of a motorcycle thanks to my brothers and the many rides I'd taken with them around the small farm where we grew up outside of Storm Lake, Iowa.

"Good God! What kind of bike is this?" I asked as Hoot backed a silver bike into my driveway. This thing was huge! It looked heavy, low to the ground, and comfortable.

"This is the Cadillac of motorcycles," he said. "It is a 1500 Honda Gold Wing, but I call it the Hooter Scooter. I thought about bringing my Harley, but it's a nice night for a long drive and the Wing is quiet. Gives us a chance to talk and enjoy the back roads."

"Are there other Hooter names?"

"Well, if I pass gas it's called a Hooter Tooter."

"Sorry I asked!"

The helmets had an intercom system so talking was easy, and the ride was like sitting in a favorite recliner on wheels. The bike was smooth and quiet as we took a long summer drive to a marina diner called Pop-N-Doc's in Decatur, NE. It was a favorite of Hoot's but a new spot for me. Their specialties were tenderloins and fried walleye.

Dinner was pleasant and the ride home was comfortable and easy. Sharing a long hug seemed natural, but he surprised me by tickling my ribs and I flinched. He smiled and said, "I'll try to remember where that spot is next time."

I was glad to hear he was interested in seeing me again, because the feeling was mutual.

"So what are you doing next weekend?" Hoot asked.

"I've got a camping trip planned."

"Somewhere local, I assume?"

"If you consider the Badlands local, then sure!"

"You're going to South Dakota? Is this a girls' trip?"

"I'm a girl, and yes, I'm going to South Dakota. I like to camp but I haven't gone anywhere in a while, so I'm headed to the Badlands. Alone."

"Do you do primitive camping? Do you have a tent? A sleeping bag? A cooler? Are you going to grill or eat out? I've got all kinds of camping equipment, what do you need?"

"Yes, I have camping equipment too, and I don't need anything, but thanks for wanting to help. And I like the idea of primitive camping, but since I'm a single woman traveling alone I'll just stay in a campground where there is some degree of safety."

After more back and forth conversation I finally agreed to use a small battery operated lantern which would be better than a flashlight for reading at night. Hoot seemed pleased to have something to offer me, perhaps because it also meant I would have to give it back at some point. In the meantime we had both indulged in the newest fad of mobile flip phones, and we stayed in touch daily for the week I was gone.

I gave him a call when I was ready to leave the campground in South Dakota and start the trip back to Iowa, and was surprised that he offered to make dinner.

"I make a great Oscar Oscar. Would you like that for dinner your first night back?"

"I have no idea what an Oscar is but two of them must be better than one. Sure, I'll come over."

After the long trip back to Iowa I went home and cleaned up, then grabbed his lantern before heading to his home across town. Pulling into his driveway for the first time I saw Hoot standing near something with smoke coming out of a top vent. I assumed it was a grill, but unlike any I'd seen before. It was big, green, and looked like a large dimpled egg. "Smells great!" I said, "but what do you call this thing?"

"It's called a Big Green Egg, or just 'the Egg.'" Raising the lid I saw filet mignon, and in his tidy, renovated kitchen he made a hollandaise sauce to put over prepared crab and asparagus on an English muffin. The Oscar Oscar meal was delicious and I recognized that there was more to Hoot than just racquetball, motorcycles, and handyman work.

"What are you doing next weekend?" he asked.

"Traveling with my brother in his semi."

"Really?"

"Yes. All of his kids, his wife, our brother, and our mom have gone with him for a week. It's my turn."

Early Monday morning of the next week my brother and I left for five days, heading from Iowa to Zeeland, MI, then on to Tulsa, OK, Little Rock, AR, and Norfolk, NE before arriving home Friday morning. The best part of the trip was having so much time with my brother, but the next best part was sitting up so high and being able to see the beautiful country. On the fourth day my brother got a notice that the standard load was cancelled, so he had some free time. We went out to eat and played pool. I had learned to play on a snooker table at home, so 8-ball was easier to play. I told Hoot about it on my next phone call.

"You play pool? Let's play sometime when you get back."

"Sure, I'd like that. I'll be back tomorrow night."

"Why don't you come over? We can have dinner and talk about the rest of the summer."

Back at Hoot's home we shared another long hug. I was expecting the tickle to my ribs, but I couldn't control my flinch. And though I was hoping for another Oscar Oscar meal, Steve had decided ordering out for pizza was on the menu. He was prepping the TV to watch Top Gun on his VCR and surround sound audio system. "Would you mind getting the pizza when they ring the bell?" he asked. "Money is on the table by the door."

"Sure, I'll take care of it."

Soon the smell of pizza, my half with Canadian bacon and his half with pepperoni and anchovies, caused him to look up. "How much was it?"

"I don't know. I gave him the money by the door like you said."

"What? I left plenty of money to cover the pizza and a tip. I didn't tell you to give it all to him!"

"Well, when I order pizza I ask how much it is and have the exact amount plus a tip ready to go. I thought everyone did it that way!"

"Oh, man. I hope I can get some of it back."

Postponing the movie we let the pizza cool while he made a few phone calls and eventually the delivery guy returned.

"Thanks for coming back," Hoot said to him.

"Yeah, I figured a $20 tip for a $12 pizza was probably a mistake."

In the meantime I learned that Hoot didn't get mad easily, and he learned to be more specific when he asked me to do something!

After the movie, he asked if I would be interested in going camping with him for a few days.

"Yes, but it won't be anytime soon. I'm taking a class for a week and then spending a few days with my mom before I head back to school in early August."

"What? School doesn't start for another month!"

"The students don't start for another month," I corrected him, "and the school counselors go back early to help with scheduling so we're ready for the students."

"Don't you have three months off?"

"I wish. From the time we wrap up the school year until we go back in the fall I have about seven weeks, so I pack a lot of things into that time."

We were able to take some short weekend camping trips before the weather put an end to warm evenings, and it was during one of these trips that I told him I was 'falling in like' with him. Soon the word 'love' was being shared between us. The mutual interests of camping, staying active, and traveling, as well as the dreams for a log cabin, were a good base for what eventually grew into a physical, exclusive relationship.

Since camping season was over we had started playing pool and while I occasionally made a few good shots, I was no match for Hoot who had teamed with his dad in pool competitions and enjoyed doing trick shots. We still played racquetball doubles three times a week until my right hip started acting up. It felt like it was burning from the inside out so I told Steve that I was going to stop playing racquetball for a while in hopes that would solve the problem.

"Do you have someone in mind to be a racquetball sub for you?" he asked.

"No, I hope I'm not gone too long, and you won't have to worry about my wild shots. I can't place the ball as well as you do."

"I'll miss you on the court, but I hope you feel better soon," he said.

About six weeks later we were discussing camping gear that we each owned and trips we had taken. Steve was grilling hamburgers on the Egg when he asked, "What would you think about taking a long camping trip?"

"What did you have in mind?"

"It's been a dream of mine to get on the bike and head west, then turn around when I get tired. What do you think? Are you willing to give up a summer to travel?"

"I can count on having the month of July off, and I enjoy traveling any direction, especially West. Is there anything special you'd like to see?"

"Since you've never been to Yellowstone, I think we could go there. And the last time I went to Mt. St. Helen's was before the volcano blew, I'd like to see it again. There's also a place called Wing Inflatables in northern California. I'd like to go there because I have an invention idea I'd like to show them."

"I'd love to see Yellowstone, and I've been to the Atlantic Ocean but not the Pacific. If we can include the ocean then yes, I'm game. Let's see if we can make it happen."

"When did you see the Atlantic?"

"My college choir took a trip to New York and the three things I really wanted to do were to stand in the ocean, see the Statue of Liberty, and get a New York bagel with cream cheese from a street vendor."

"Mission accomplished?"

"Yes, but everything on that trip was an experience. I've also spent about ten days in Ireland with a teacher friend. My favorite part there was going to a small pub off the beaten path. It had a large fireplace, sawdust on the floor and two musicians were playing. One had a bass flute and the other had a large hand drum. It's one of my favorite musical memories."

"Why did you go to Ireland?" Hoot asked.

"I was in my first year of teaching, 1984, in a small town called Melrose, Minnesota. One of the other teachers was also in her first year. Her grandparents owned a home in Ireland and as a college graduation gift they offered to let her spend a summer in their home when they were gone. She could invite a friend for ten days, so she invited me. I had never flown before so an international flight was a big deal."

"Did she know the area? How did you get around?"

"Her grandparents were good friends with the neighbors who took us under their wing. My friend had a driver's license valid for Ireland which was fine with me since they drive on the opposite side of the road."

"I like to travel, but I'm not interested in anything like New York or international sights. There's plenty to see here in the states and I always go west. There's too many people out east, and more natural beauty in the west."

"Nature is wonderful, but any travel can be a good experience, even if the experience is to learn I never want to go back somewhere again!"

"No argument there!" Hoot said.

Chapter 2
Trip Plans

Around Christmas I knew I couldn't keep quiet about a problem that wasn't going away. "Hey, Hoot, I think I need to see someone about my right hip."

"Why? I thought it was getting better."

"It goes in waves. Sometimes it's fine, but when it hurts it really painful."

"I'm not a fan of doctors." Hoot said. "I think you just need to do some stretches and maybe start exercising again."

"Maybe. It's the worst when I move from sitting to standing, and getting out of the car is starting to be a problem."

"Can you ride the bike? What about our trip next summer?"

"The bike is put away for the winter, so I'm not sure if I can ride or not, and I'm aware of our summer plans but this pain is not going away. Why don't you like doctors?"

"I know my body. I take reasonably good care of it, and see a chiropractor once in a while. If there's a problem no one else can understand exactly how I feel, so why should I pay someone else a bunch of money when he is making a best guess at what's going on. Besides, do you have any idea what insurance costs when you're self-employed?"

"How do you assume this chiropractor knows how you feel?"

"I've known this guy for years and I trust him."

"OK. So you don't have health insurance?"

"Nope, and I haven't needed it, either. Someday I might have a problem with my health but I'll deal with it when it happens."

"When's the last time you've been to a doctor?"

"Probably about 10 years."

"Ten years?! How about a dentist?"

"Probably about 10 years. Anyway, we were talking about your leg. If you go to a doctor what do you think they would do to help you?"

"I'm not sure, but this problem isn't going away."

"It sounds like stretches are all you need, but you have insurance so I guess it couldn't hurt to see a doctor."

Seeing my family doctor resulted in a diagnosis of bursitis, and a script for prescription strength ibuprofen.

"How much did that cost you?" Hoot wanted to know.

"My co-pay was $20 for the doctor visit, and $5 for the meds."

"I hope it works. Let's keep thinking about our summer trip."

In the meantime, I checked in with my mom. "What kind of surgery did Dad have on his back?" I asked.

"His family has a history of bad backs," Mom explained, "and when he started having trouble he tried a number of things to help, but ended up having surgery in August of 1965. He was 43 years old. The surgery was on his low back to address spinal stenosis which is a narrowing of the spine that compresses the nerves. They took a bone graft from his leg to stabilize his back while it healed and had to wear a brace on his leg. I remember him saying the leg was more painful after surgery than his back. We had neighbors help with the chores and the harvest that year since he needed time to heal. I still remember all the farmers coming to do the field work, and the colors of the tractors that were in the farmyard. It was quite a sight and an incredible help that year."

"I hope I don't need surgery," I told her. "I'm not sure that bursitis is the problem, but I'm trying to do what's right."

"I hope you don't need surgery, either," Mom said. "And I also hope that Steve is helping you since you're having trouble getting around."

"Yes, he is. He's making meals for me to put in the freezer so I don't have to work in the kitchen. There's not much else he can do except take the pain away and he can't do that."

"I'm glad he's there to help," Mom said.

Returning to the doctor later I explained that not only did my hip hurt, but I was having shooting pain down my right leg. This resulted in an appointment with a different doctor for a cortisone shot in my hip.

"Do you ski?" Hoot asked one day.

"Just on bunny hills, why do you ask?"

"I'm going on a ski trip with some of my buddies. Would you want to come along? Maybe the exercise and clean air would help with your leg."

"I'm not going to take a chance with my leg

because I really want to take that trip this summer. I have an appointment for a cortisone shot, so maybe that will help."

"Seems like a lot of money you're shelling out without much to show for it," Hoot remarked. "It's already March and we're planning on the trip in July."

I went to the appointment while Steve was on the ski trip, but I didn't get the shot.

"What happened?" Hoot asked.

"This new doctor had the shot ready to go. I was on the exam table, face down. I was really hurting because it's hard to lay flat. I could feel him touching my hip. He asked me at one point 'does this hurt?'

"Nothing hurt more than usual and the doctor asked 'are you sure?'"

I asked him, "Is it supposed to hurt?"

"He said 'I'm squeezing the bursa in my fingers. If you had bursitis I would have to peel you off the ceiling. You do not have bursitis."

"So now what?" Steve asked.

"Next step is an MRI to see what is causing the problem in my leg."

"I'll be back in a few days so I'll see you soon."

"Evidently I have spinal stenosis," I told Hoot after the MRI. "Just like my dad had in an area of the low back called the lumbar. Did you know the vertebrae are numbered? I have problems with the squishy gel substances between vertebrae 4-5 and 5-6. The nerves have already been damaged because so much time has passed, and if I keep going at this rate the damage will only get worse."

"Surgery?" Hoot asked.

"It looks that way, although they want to do more tests."

"So your first doctor diagnosed you and treated you for the wrong thing, and during that time your spinal stenosis problem created nerve damage, do I have that right?"

"Sounds right."

"Sounds like medical malpractice to me."

"That thought crossed my mind, too, but I can't imagine the time and money involved in a malpractice allegation, and I hurt too much to worry about it. I just want the pain to go away."

"I think situations like yours are why doctors have malpractice insurance."

"I'm not going to go there."

"I don't agree with you on that, but I do agree it would probably be a hassle trying to prove it. So you're not going to consider malpractice but you are going to let them cut on your spinal column?"

"Do you know how you always say, 'I know my body the best and no one knows how I feel except me?' Well, you don't know how much I'm hurting. The fact that this is a trait in my family helps me know it's probably something I was born with, not because of an especially hard racquetball game, or tripping on a sidewalk. I'm not even sitting at work anymore. The custodians built me a standing desk. The most difficult part of my job is the 30 mile drive to and from work because sitting is so painful. Something else that is painful is when you tickle my ribs. I always flinch and flinching hurts. Could you please stop?"

"Yes, I can stop. But if I forget and do it anyway it really will be because I forgot."

"Understood," I said.

Hoot continued to express concern about an unnecessary surgery and asked if I could have my scans sent to the chiropractor he trusted. The chiropractor told Hoot that based on the pictures, I was one of the small percentage of people who would probably need surgery to fix the problem. After that, Hoot was supportive, but we kept an eye on the calendar. It was now April. What about our trip planned for July?

My next doctor visit was to a neurosurgeon. "Well, Mary, you have a problem. I can fix this for you and fortunately we no longer need to do bone grafts from your leg. However I do have an unusual requirement for recuperation. I don't want you to sit for one month after surgery."

My stunned expression replaced my need for words.

"The spinal column is like a rubber band. I will be repairing a weak spot in the rubber band." he explained. "When we sit, we create tension in the rubber band and the repair would struggle to heal. If you can avoid sitting, like you've already been doing, then the 'rubber band' will have time to heal in a relaxed position, you will have very little scar tissue, and you'll be good to go."

"How do I function? I avoid sitting now, but sometimes I don't have a choice."

"You can stand, kneel, walk or lay for four weeks, with brief sitting for meals or bathroom use. But if you can put up with the inconvenience of not sitting for four weeks, you will reap the benefits for the rest of your life."

Hoot and I had been talking about our July trip for the past year and suddenly it was in jeopardy. Surgery took place without incident at the end of the school year in late May 2000 when I was 38 years old. Hoot set up a daybed in the basement of my split level home, and I rented a big screen TV in a huge cabinet. Steve made sure I had plenty of VCR movies to watch, and he made library runs for me when I called in a list of books I wanted to read. I took frequent walks in the early summer weather. At the end of the 4 weeks Hoot drove me back to the neurosurgeon while I laid in the back seat of his extended cab truck.

"Congratulations, Mary! Everything looks great!" the surgeon said. "I'm sure not sitting was awkward, but you will have very little scar tissue. You can start sitting again in small doses as much as you can tolerate. Steve, I'm sure you have been a big help. Do either of you have any questions?"

Glancing at each other I gave Steve a nod, and taking a deep breath he said, "Doc, Mary and I have been planning a motorcycle trip since last fall. We had hoped to be gone for the month of July, leaving in about 10 days. She hasn't sat for 30 days. Is this even possible?"

"What kind of bike do you have?" the surgeon asked.

"Honda Gold Wing 1500," Hoot replied.

Giving Hoot's shoulder a squeeze the neurosurgeon smiled and said, "Have a good trip!"

The tension that had been building about our tenuous plans was released in laughter.

"But," the surgeon continued, shaking his finger in Hoot's face, "Mary has had major surgery and hasn't sat in 4 weeks. She has exercises to do. When she starts feeling tightness in her back she will tell you to pull over and you have to do that, understand?"

"Yessir," Hoot said.

"And Mary," the surgeon turned to me, "no more racquetball. I do encourage you to exercise but the twisting and sudden stops in racquetball is not a good idea for you. The spot that I fixed won't be a problem, but you don't want the nearby areas in your back to start acting up."

"Yessir," I said. I was sad to say goodbye to racquetball but didn't ever want to go through this ordeal again.

The next week flew by as we started packing the Bushtec motorcycle trailer with camping gear, electric clothing (like an electric blanket, but worn under a jacket) that we would wear in the mountains, cooking utensils and a variety of other equipment. I learned that crunchy peanut butter was mandatory, not only for a quick energy snack on the road, but because Hoot ate it with every breakfast and most restaurants don't have the crunchy variety. I made it a point to do my exercises and gradually got used to sitting for increasingly longer periods of time. Pulling out of Sioux City on Friday, July 7, 2000, I was surprised that a few of Hoot's motorcycle buddies rode with us the first 100 miles. It was news to me that it's a typical thing biker friends do for each other at the beginning of a long trip. It seemed that it was more likely a good excuse for guys to ride, but it was a nice send off.

The surgeon was right that every few hours I tapped Hoot on the shoulder, expecting that he would find a spot to pull over in the next few miles. Imagine my surprise when he pulled over immediately on the side of the road and helped me off the bike.

"You could wait a few miles," I said. "The side of the road isn't comfortable for doing my stretches, even using the sleeping pad for a cushion."

"You have two brothers, a mother and a neurosurgeon that I'll need to answer to if anything happens to you on this trip," Hoot explained. "I'm not taking any chances!"

As we continued on the trip I found I could stay seated for longer periods of time and soon I only did my stretches whenever we made fuel stops. Hoot found that he could tickle my ribs again without needing to worry that it would hurt me, and like always, I flinched.

Chapter 3
Trip #1 - July 2000

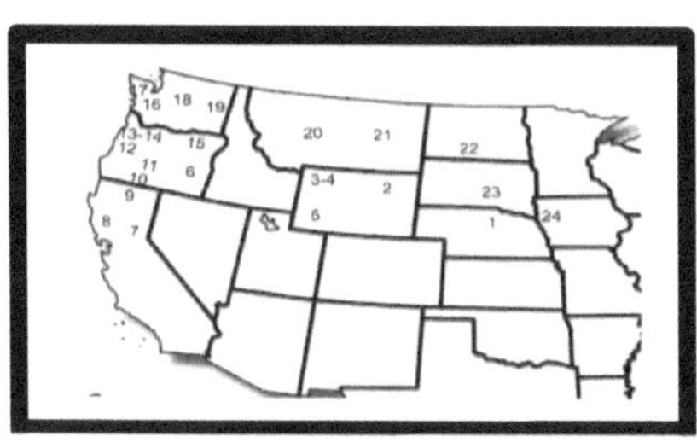

1	Valentine, NE		13, 14	Newport, OR
2	Buffalo, WY		15	Cascade Lockes, OR
3, 4	Yellowstone, WY		16	Shelton, WA
5	Jackson Hole, WY		17	Port Angeles, WA
6	Ontario, OR		18	Winthrop, WA
7	Whiskey Creek, CA		19	Newport, WA
8	Eureka, CA		20	Big Fort Village, MT
9	Burnt Ranch, CA		21	Havre, MT
10	Ashland, OR		22	Gillette, ND
11	Gold Hill, OR		23	Pierre, SD
12	Coos Bay, OR		24	Sioux City, IA (home)

The interstate is an efficient way to get from point A to point B, but I soon learned that Hoot didn't like to travel by interstate. Eventually I appreciated his preference for using the back roads and scenic byways which were much more interesting and less stressful. The trip was amazing and such a change from the routine of bells and hallways and teenagers.

"So what are your first thoughts about Yellowstone?" Hoot asked as we set up the tent in the campground, taking care to secure food so bears wouldn't visit overnight.

"It's breathtaking! If I didn't already believe the earth was shifting below our feet then I wouldn't have been able to argue after today. Old Faithful was as amazing as I had expected, and the sulfur springs stink! But this day alone is worth the trip."

"We're just getting started! Don't even think about going home yet!" Hoot said.

As we were leaving the park the next day we saw a bear on the side of the road and it drove home the point that we were on a bike with no exterior protection. "Take your picture and let's go!" Hoot said, and we headed further west.

While many people talk about Jackson Hole, WY, and the Grand Tetons as amazing places, I found that my favorite spot was Hoback Junction, WY. The beauty there spoke to me in a way no other place on the trip had to that point.

"Log cabin territory?" Hoot asked.

"Definitely," I replied.

"Let's add it to the list."

"We have a list?"

"We do now!"

Southern Idaho was like a desert and the road was deserted. Hoot cranked the tunes and I stood up on the bike, carefully, and danced. We enjoyed trying to identify the various crops growing in the fields including potatoes, onions, wheat, cabbage, lettuce, and many others. Quite a change from corn, beans, and alfalfa in Iowa.

The time on the road also provided opportunities for some long talks, and marriage was occasionally the topic. "I was married once for about a year a long time ago," Hoot said. "It didn't work out, and I'm not sure I want to get married again. I burned that card."

I was curious to know more about that, but decided to wait before asking any questions.

"Well, I've never been married and don't want to live together unless we're married," I replied.

"I don't want to live together either. We're both pretty independent. We've got a good thing going now," he reminded me, "Why change it? We have plenty of time. Let's see how things go on this trip with nothing to distract us, and we can always talk about marriage later. And you should probably know that I don't do well with ultimatums."

"Message received," I said.

Ending the day near the ocean we wandered into a toy store, bought a two string flexi-foil kite and flew it on the beach of the Pacific. How freeing this all was!

"What are you doing?" Hoot asked one evening. You sure are busy writing every night."

"I'm keeping track of our days and our route," I explained. "I want to make a scrapbook of our trip."

"You mean like a photo album?"

"Kind of, but scrapbooking is a new craft and it's a big jump from photo albums. I want to make a scrapbook of this trip when we get home."

"OK, but it sounds like a glorified photo album to me."

"You'll see," I replied.

At one point, in Oregon, we were riding along and Hoot saw a John Deere implement dealer selling combines, tractors and other assorted farming equipment. Being a farm kid and enjoying machines, he pulled into the dealership and said he wouldn't be long. A sales rep came out and they started looking at the new machinery, and the latest gadgets and improvements to equipment. Being at a farm implement dealership isn't much different than being at a car dealership. There isn't much to look at except equipment and related accessories. I stayed near the bike, took off a layer of my clothing and did my exercises, and eventually wandered into the shop which held the accessories, and odds and ends for farmers. I grew up on a farm and was familiar with what they were selling, but I had no use for engine parts, cab umbrellas, and slow moving vehicle reflective signs. The sales clerk gave me a knowing smile and asked if I wanted a cup of coffee. After 45 minutes Hoot finally returned and as we got back on the road he was telling me about how GPS worked, all the GPS options on the equipment he had just seen, and the driverless farm machinery that was starting to be sold.

That night we were camped at Newport, Oregon, and went into town for dinner and to wander in the stores. I stopped in a gift store, and Hoot followed me in. I was looking at marine related items and after ten minutes Hoot said, "I don't mind being here, but if you're going to buy something, then do it. If not, then let's go."

I looked at him for a moment and asked "How many tractors did you buy in the 45 minutes that you were looking at John Deere equipment today?"

His face turned red. "Take your time," he said. "I'll wait outside." I thought the sales clerk would choke on her laughter!

The next day we checked out a quiet antique store because the upright piano just inside the door had caught my eye. I've played piano for years so I sat down, opened up the sheet music of old musicals sitting on the bench and started playing. I was surprised the piano was almost in tune. Soon other people started wandering in and the store was getting busy. The manager stopped by and said "Please don't stop playing, you're really helping my business!" He handed me a gift card for a nearby restaurant, so we used it for lunch.

"It never occurred to me that something like playing piano could be so useful," Hoot said at the end of the meal.

"I can't fix things like you can," I replied, "but the money I make from giving piano lessons, or playing and singing can help me afford things including random meals for lunch or air conditioner repairs. One of my more unusual experiences is playing piano at a local bar every year on St. Patrick's day. I get paid, I get free drinks, and after the first hour I charge $5 each time someone wants to sing Danny Boy. I make a lot in tips! Otherwise I play at church, or play background music for dinner parties and things like that. I enjoy it!"

I had warned Hoot that I also like to quilt, and that I can usually sniff out fabric stores. Sure enough, I found a store and purchased beautiful earth tone fabrics that I thought would make a nice quilt as a gift for Hoot. He liked the colors and I was grateful we were pulling a trailer so there was room for some purchases, although Hoot commented that it created extra weight in the trailer. He claimed he could feel the extra weight when we got back on the road. I didn't feel the difference and couldn't imagine that a few yards of fabric would be noticeable. I figured if I were in a car I wouldn't notice a few yards of fabric in the trunk, but motorcycles are not cars, and I would eventually need to reconsider my opinion about the extra weight.

We wandered into another toy store and walked out with a monkey puppet with an extra long tail. We named the monkey Charlie and with my help he would entertain kids in the vehicles that we passed on the road. I had Charlie crawl up Hoot's back, or nuzzle him on the neck, or just pretend to fly in the wind. Hoot joined in the fun and would reach back to scratch Charlie's head. A few times the cars slowed down to keep pace with us and wave at Charlie. That little puppet helped provide a break in some of the long days on the road.

"Hey Hoot?" I asked, breaking the silence one day.

"You're awake?" he asked. "You were so quiet I thought you fell asleep!"

"No, I was thinking about everything you own.

How do you afford all of it?"

"Like what?" he asked.

"Like two apartment buildings and a house for starters. Two large motorcycles and a nice truck, and all your woodworking tools. I know that the rent from the apartment buildings would help to pay back the bank loans that you probably took out in order to buy them, but I don't see where you get your money. Some people have one or two expensive hobbies, but you seem to have money for numerous hobbies, and can get whatever you want. I'm not asking for banking details, but I'm curious."

"I could make up a hell of a story here, but the simple truth is that I am frugal but not cheap. I used to work for a boss and have had a few jobs that paid me well. I saved my money and was able to eventually become my own boss."

"Why did you quit your jobs?"

"I don't like working for someone else who tells me when to work and how to work. I prefer the freedom, and responsibility, of working for myself."

"What do you mean about not being cheap?"

"I like nice things, but I'm picky about what I spend my money on. I buy the best I can afford of the things I want. Like this Hooter Scooter we're riding. It is the best touring bike that money can buy. When I was researching smokers and grills the Big Green Egg was at the top of the list for what I wanted. I could have bought the cabinet it sits in, they call it The Nest, but I built a cabinet instead. The Egg is what was important, not the cabinet it sits in."

"That makes sense," I said.

"When I started living on my own it didn't take too

long to figure out that if I wanted to eat I needed to learn how to cook. Cooking for one is pretty cheap."

"I sure benefit from your cooking. You make great meals!"

"And you make great desserts. We make a good team," he said. "Does that answer your question?"

"Yes, and that probably explains why you keep your thermostat low in the winter, right?"

"Yup. Just wear a sweater if you're cold. Paying a low heating bill in the winter allows for more spending money in the summer to go on vacation!"

Traveling down another quiet highway Hoot had a question for me. "Why don't you talk much about school? I know you spend a lot of time there, and you make comments once in a while, but you don't talk about it much. I've often wondered why you don't share more about what goes on."

"Two reasons. First, when I get home I don't want to relive my school day because I want to leave it at school. I'm usually exhausted when I get home because I feel like I have whiplash from switching gears all day. Think of it like customer service at a store. Every person that comes in the door needs something different. I might start the morning talking to a parent concerned about their child, then a student comes in to ask about registering for classes next year, then another student is crying because someone said something mean to them, or a student skipped first period and the principal needs me to check bathrooms to look for her. And I haven't even read my emails yet. That can all be within the first 20 minutes of the day. Some of the things I deal with are pretty heavy and I'm glad to leave it at school."

"I suppose I can understand why you wouldn't want to relive all of that," Hoot said. "What's the other reason?"

"The other reason is that much of my work is confidential and it's just easier to keep everything private instead of trying to sift between what I can tell you or not."

"It's not like I'm going to know anyone at your school," Hoot said.

"True, but if I don't say anything then there's no chance that you could innocently share something that could get traced back to me. Overall my day involves three main areas of focus: career, academics, and social emotional."

"Examples, please. We have an open road ahead of us and plenty of time."

"Alright, so I teach a career class for 4 ½ weeks to our 8th graders. I set it up so that during our time together they have to identify a career they are interested in and then I try to line up a half day job shadow for them. They have to do some research before they go, and give a short report when they return."

"That sounds like a good idea. What are some of the jobs they shadow?"

"There are very common requests, usually things their parents do, or something they've seen or heard about, but there were two that were most memorable. One of them was a girl who was determined to be a vet. It's all she talked about, so I lined up a half day with the local vet. She came back the next day and was pretty quiet. When she had to give her report to the class she didn't want to say anything. I had no idea what had happened but she finally said that they had to make a farm call to help a sow that was having trouble delivering her litter of pigs."

"I know where this is headed," Hoot said.

"We're both farm kids, and yeah, you're exactly right. The girl finally explained to the class that the vet had to put on a long rubber glove and reach in to find the problem. I thought she was going to throw up at the memory. But she seemed to feel better when I suggested she could be a small animal vet in a large city where farm visits wouldn't be part of the job."

"Sounds like a good experience for her," Steve said.

"Yeah, a career class should be about exposure to real life, so kids have to shake my hand and greet me when they walk into class. We practice filling out job applications. I also make them count back change to me. I have such a short time in class and I try to make the most of it."

"How do you make them count back change?"

"I use monopoly money for the bills and have a few dollars in real coins. Then I have about 20 index cards with a variety of situations. Kids pull a card, read the situation and have to count back the change. For example, the card could say: you have a part time job delivering pizza and the total comes to $22.65. They give you $30.00. Count back the change."

"Well, what if somebody just gives them a pile of money and takes the pizza, like you did last year?" Hoot asked with a chuckle in his voice.

"Actually the kids ask if they could keep the change as a tip, but I make them count the change back anyway. I know people are using credit cards more often, but counting back change is a dying art and I think it's helpful to know."

"No argument there," Hoot said. "What was the other memorable job shadow?"

"A boy who wanted to work with a plumber."

"Good for him! Learn a trade!" Hoot said.

"Right, but when he came back and gave his report he had a similar experience as the girl. They had been called to a home with a backed up toilet."

"Uh oh, I've had experience with that. I'm guessing it backed up into the tub?"

"Yup. The kid said there was no way he was going to be a plumber, but then I reminded him that people will pay just about anything for someone to fix that problem so if he has that skill then he could name his price."

"Sounds like your career class is pretty realistic."

"I hope so. My first job was catching nightcrawlers, and I learned the value of a dollar at a young age. I think it's important for kids to experience what people do for work and that the money doesn't just appear in a bank account."

"What's the story of the nightcrawlers?"

"When I was about eight years old we would go to town once a week for groceries and errands. In the summer my parents would drop me off at the pool so I could hang out with my school friends who lived in town. They had a season pass, but I paid each time I went and the cost was a quarter. Dad always gave me the money. One year the price went up ten cents. I mentioned it to my dad and he said "Honey, it's time you learn about inflation. I'll still give you a quarter, but it's up to you to add the extra ten cents."

"I didn't know what I was going to do! The only money I had was from a few gifts during the year and to say my piggy bank was skinny was an understatement. One day my brothers went to town, and Mom made them take me along. They went into a store that sold fishing bait and there was a sign on the door that said nightcrawlers needed at .75 per dozen. All of sudden I knew I'd be going to the pool all summer! Dad helped me by going out in the cool evening or after a rain to pick up wood or lumber, then shine the flashlight. I got pretty quick in grabbing the nightcrawlers were hiding. I made a lot of money that summer and learned the value of a dollar. I've had some type of job ever since then."

"That was a good lesson your dad taught you."

"Yes, it was. Even though I was little, there was still something I could do to earn a few dollars if I was willing to work for it."

"So what else do you do during the day?"

"Well, I work in a school so academics are pretty standard conversations. I help kids who struggle with their work or are so advanced that they're bored. I help them look at careers they might be interested in and map out high school courses that could lead them in the direction they want to go."

"You help kids with math and English and biology work?"

"No, I don't usually help them with their work, but I can help them organize their calendar, or show them how a few more percentage points can boost their grade, or just give them a pep talk. Sometimes I work with other teachers to support a struggling student or do something different for a student who already has mastered the content and is looking for something more challenging.

"Yeah, that brings back some memories. So what is the other part of your job? Emotional something?"

"Social emotional."

"Drama?" Hoot suggested.

"Sometimes. That's the hardest part of my job because it's different for every student, and it's not tangible like a job shadow or percentage points of a grade. Sometimes kids are struggling with problems at home, or a break up with their significant other, or questioning their sexuality or once in a while a student will wonder about the point of living."

"What do you do with all of that?"

"I always start by just letting the student talk. They usually have a lot on their mind and by the time they come to talk to me it's something they've mulled over on their own. Sometimes I have an answer for them, but usually I just provide support. There are some situations where I have to call home, like if a student is asking about 'what's the point of living.'"

"Huh. I never thought about kids having those kind of thoughts. I figured your kids would more likely complain about being bullied."

"That happens too, but it's a lot more than that."

We let the conversation sit quietly for a few miles, then I continued. "Actually there's this kid that has been on my mind a lot. A teacher asked me to talk to one of the girls because she's at school by 6:30 AM."

"That seems early," Hoot said. "Is the teacher there that early?"

"Yes, some teachers stay late and some come early. My boss said he's usually at school by 5:00 AM because it's the only time of the day he has a chance to get uninterrupted work done."

"There's probably not many kids there by 6:30 though, right?"

"Correct, but I was that kid, too. My mom had to be at work by 6:30 and the public school bus wasn't allowed to pick up the Catholic school kids so I went into town with my mom. I was at school by 6:30 and would often practice piano early in the morning, and eventually I started playing organ for the 7:00 church service, but this girl doesn't play piano."

"So what was going on with her?"

"She qualifies to ride the bus, but doesn't want to, so her dad gives her a ride. She does her homework early in the morning."

"So what happened?" Hoot asked.

"I checked in with her. Nothing much seemed to be a problem on the surface, but it's just she and her dad at home and evidently things get kind of tense once in a while. She's a chatterbox and in the middle of a conversation she asked if I would adopt her. That's a strange comment. I'm going to check in on her occasionally."

"Where's the mom?"

"Evidently her mom walked out many years ago and hasn't been back."

"What's her name?" Hoot wanted to know.

"I rarely talk about student situations and never share student names, but let's call her Caprice."

"OK."

"She's a neat kid. She's on my mind because of her

comment about adoption but there's no reason for me to do anything about it other than to check in with her once in a while."

By this time we were nearing Arcata, California where a company called Wing Inflatables was located. Hoot had called ahead to talk to someone at Wing about an idea he had. Hoot was a gadget guy and loved to come up with new ways of doing things. He had created a prototype for an idea of using compressed air and tire inner tubes to quickly inflate a tent instead of fighting with tent poles, or to use in a larger scale by construction crews during the winter rather than building the wood frames and plastic sheeting typically used. We toured Wing to see about the possibility of turning Hoot's prototype into something more. The owner was interested in what Hoot was suggesting and they discussed materials and processes, but ultimately Hoot decided to put the idea on hold. Then we were invited to a white water rafting trip on the Trinity River with level 2 and 3 runs using some of the heavy duty rubber rafts which they built at Wing. I wasn't allowed to help with paddling because of my recent back surgery, so I just hung on to the boat and enjoyed the ride!

Attending a Catholic church service on Sunday is important to me, and as a church musician I enjoy hearing how other church musicians provide music, so we found a Mission church near Hoopa, CA. It remains one of the most significant services I have ever attended. The music was nondescript, but nothing on the outside gave any indication of the warmth, character and Native American spirituality on the inside. Hoot rarely attended church but accompanied me to this service and we both noted that it was not a typical church setting. The vessel that held the communion wafers was a turtle shell, and the stations of the cross were of Native Americans in traditional garb and tepee shelters. The 25 people in the pews looked at us as curiosities, but they were very welcoming and had many questions for Hoot about his bike after the service.

A few days later we found white sand dunes on the coast and rented ATVs to go dune-bugging. The general safety instructions from the manager at the rental store explained that the ATV brake pedal was activated by pushing down with the right foot. I didn't think the nerve damage in my right leg would be a problem until I started getting a lot of speed going up a dune. I tried to apply the brake but I couldn't make my leg work the way it needed to, so I ended up going way too fast and went airborne. I had learned from riding a bike over hills on the farm that you should stand with knees bent so when the bike hits the ground you probably won't get hurt. Fortunately the same concept applied to dune buggies. Hoot said later that the wheels of my dune buggy had been at least four feet in the air. He was sure he was going to have to find an emergency room for me, and had been trying to figure out how he was going to explain this to my mom.

"This reminds me of a saying I've heard," Hoot said after I was sure I didn't cause any damage. "Do you know the greatest thrill known to man?

"I'll bite," I said. "I assume it's flying?"

"No. Flying is the second greatest thrill. Landing is the first!"

"Did you come up with that on your own?" I asked.

"No. I'm sure someone else coined the phrase, but I don't know who gets the credit."

At one point we took a chartered salmon fishing trip about an hour's ride into the Pacific Ocean. When we got a bite we were supposed to yell "Fish on!" and one of the crew would run to help us land the salmon. Pretty soon I had a bite. I yelled, "Fish out!" I'm not sure who laughed more, Hoot or the crew. Having a fish out of the water seemed to be the same as having a fish on the line, so in my mind it didn't matter what I yelled, but evidently there's a difference. We had four salmon to show for our efforts, the maximum allowed, and typically the charter company would ship them to our homes in dry ice. We had no idea when we would be home so we opted to give the salmon to a local restaurant in exchange for an evening meal. It was a good trade.

Then we drove to Mt. St. Helens which erupted the morning of my high school graduation, May 18, 1980. We were driving in heavy fog and weren't able to see the volcano, but the incredible devastation of the area was impossible to miss. One of the most notable images of the explosion is that all the trees fell in the same direction with their roots pointing toward the volcano. Later in the day we stopped at a lounge called DooWop in Shelton, WA. where we played a few games of pool. I enjoy the game, but I'm no good. Hoot, however, is a pool shark. Usually he uses the opportunity to help me play better, but a local college aged kid had challenged Hoot so I just watched as Steve played the first game with him casually, then pulled out all the stops on the next two. I felt sorry for the kid who looked like a sad puppy as he left.

Arriving in Port Angeles we went bowling and ate at Pizza Hut, both things we would do at home. We took it as a sign that it was time to work our way back toward Iowa. On the way we took a ferry ride and then traveled through the North Cascades and Glacier National Park. They were beautiful! That was followed by touring the Grand Coulee Dam. All of these places were so large that my camera just couldn't do justice to the size and grandeur of what we were seeing. We had a few more days of travel before we pulled into Iowa.

"Want to see the scrapbook?" I asked Steve about six weeks later.

"This is really nice," he said as he studied the pages. "I can see that you used the notes you took each day. Are you going to do this next summer, too?"

"Sure, where are we going?"

"I don't know yet, but let's think about it. Hopefully you won't have any health problems next spring!"

"Speaking of health problems, I've noticed that sometimes you don't finish what you start in bed," I said. "Everything OK? Do you want to look into getting some Viagra?"

"I know, I'm sorry. I'm just too tired by the time we get to bed. I'm fine."

"It seems like you are getting up more often in the night to pee, too."

"Are you keeping track?" he asked.

"No, but it's obvious when we sleep in a tent."

"Hey, at least I get up in time! Imagine this conversation if I didn't get out of the tent before taking care of business."

"Well, I wanted to ask. I care about you."

"Thanks. I'm fine, nothing to worry about."

Now that we were back home we settled into a familiar routine. Hoot worked on his rental properties, I kept busy at school during the day, worked on his quilt at night, and we usually spent weekends together.

"Between your job and mine, we don't see each other very often," Steve commented while grilling Iowa chops one Friday night. "I know we usually see each other at the gym every morning, but the ten miles between our homes makes a difference.

"If we were married we'd live closer together," I said, raising an eyebrow.

"On the other hand, we see each other every weekend and that's enough for now." He paused, then said, "I know we should probably talk about marriage sometime, but I'm just not ready to have that conversation. We'll get to it later," and returned his attention back to the chops.

Chapter 4
Trip #2 - July 2001

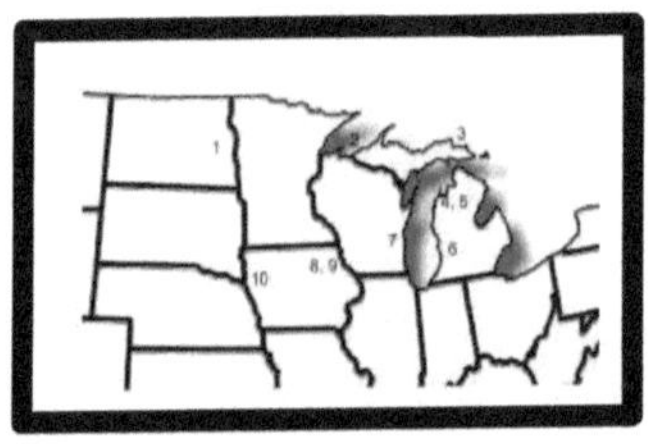

We traveled 2,580 miles in 10 days on the Goldwing 1800.
The numbers represent where each day ended.
It rained almost every day, but we still had fun!

1	Grand Forks, ND		6	Elberta, MI
2	Thunder Bay, Ontario Province		7	Manitowa, WI
3	Wawa, Ontario Province		8,9	Kendaville, IA
4, 5	Mackinaw City, MI		10	Sioux City, IA (home)

"What do you think about checking out the U.P.?" Hoot asked one snowy winter day.

"Sure. What's the UP? Is it a new restaurant in town?"

"No, goofball, the U.P. is the Upper Peninsula in Michigan. Have you heard of Mackinaw Island?"

"Yes, and I've heard of the Upper Peninsula, I've just never heard it called the U.P".

Getting an atlas, Hoot and I spent the next few months studying options for a summer trip. After considering various destinations we decided to head to the U.P. in July, and we would pull the trailer since we planned to camp. Hoot had traded in the silver 1500 Goldwing for a new metallic blue 1800 Goldwing, and I had to admit that I could tell the difference when pulling the trailer because the engine didn't work any harder with the trailer than without it. It was a noticeable difference from the 1500 we had used the previous summer, so I conceded that he might have felt the difference those few yards of fabric had made last year.

We learned from our West Coast trip that we tended to eat twice a day so the crunchy peanut butter came along but the pots and pans stayed home and we stopped at local restaurants along the road.

"Do you know how to find the best place for breakfast in a small town?" Hoot asked one morning.

"I'll bite," I said. "How do you know where the best place is for breakfast?"

"Look for a lot of pickup trucks parked outside."

That advice served us well, but the most distinctive part of the entire trip was the weather. It rained every single day of the trip, and the farther north we went the cooler it got. By the time we pulled into our campsite in Wawa, Canada, we were wearing our heated electric clothing covered by long sleeved t-shirts, sweat shirts, coats and rain gear. We got some strange looks from the people warm and dry in their RV's.

"You've been kind of quiet," Hoot said that evening. "You've either turned into an ice cube or something's on your mind. Which is it?"

"The electric clothing kept my core warm so I'm not an ice cube, but I am thinking about our birthdays next year. I'm turning 40 in February and you're turning 50 in September. Any thoughts about celebrations?"

"It might be hard to beat some of the previous celebrations," Hoot said. "I really liked the hour of flight time you got me last year. It was great to be back up in the air again, even if it had to be with an instructor."

"Thanks, you kept talking about how much you liked to fly but since you sold your plane and let your license lapse I thought an hour would be fun. I'm glad you liked it! And I liked heading south last February to hear a bluegrass festival for my birthday. But it would be nice to do something significant for your 50th."

"We've got more than a year to think about my 50th," Hoot said. "The one thing I know for sure is that neither of us like surprises. It's only July. We've got lots of time to talk about it later."

Our time in the U.P. was amazing. Everything was so clean and not having any motor vehicles on Mackinaw Island made me appreciate the clean air we take so for granted. They used horses and bicycles for transportation, and I watched a teenager clean up the horse poop on the street. "I want to tell kids about this in the career class I teach," I said to Hoot. "I doubt this is a desirable job but I hope it pays well, and it's a good response to the kids who complain about getting up early to deliver newspapers!"

"Speaking of kids, how is that girl doing?"

It took me a moment to realize he meant Caprice.

"She's had a hard year, and it sounds like things are getting tough with her dad. She keeps asking me and other teachers to adopt her. That's unusual."

"Sounds like a spoiled brat who doesn't want to follow the rules and dad's just being a good parent."

"Well, all I know for sure is that neither of us live in her home to really know what's happening. All I have to go on is what she tells me."

"Lots of kids complain about their parents," Hoot said.

"Yes, but when parents get physical with their kids, then the school system pays closer attention."

"He spanks her?"

"No, at least I don't think so. I think he grabs her by the arms but it's hard to tell. She has started wearing oversized t-shirts so I wonder if she's hiding something. She likes to play softball and the coach told me that Caprice really hustles which can sometimes cause deep bruises on her arms and legs."

"Sounds possible," Hoot said.

"Yes, until the bruises look like they were made by fingers."

"That happened?"

"Yes. I didn't see a bruise until she moved her hair out of her eyes and her sleeve exposed her upper arm so I noticed it then. And when she tells me that she moves the dresser in front of her door at night then she's definitely got my attention."

"What do you do then?"

"Any time I have reasonable suspicion of abuse I

have to call the authorities."

"Police?"

"No, an organization called DHS which means Department of Human Services. Some states call it CPS which means Child Protection Services. Every state has their own system. They've been called a few times based on things Caprice has said in class or has told me."

"Do you have to be the one to call?"

"No, whoever has the suspicion that there's a problem is the person who calls. Sometimes it's me, sometimes it's a classroom teacher. It needs to be the person with first hand knowledge of what they saw or heard. So a teacher can't tell me what Caprice said and then ask me to call DHS, but I can sit with the teacher when they make the call."

"Why would you sit with the teacher?"

"It's not unusual for counselors to call DHS, but teachers might only do it a few times in their career. They get nervous, so I'll offer to sit with them. They usually take me up on the offer."

"So what happens after the phone call?"

"If the report meets DHS criteria then someone from that department will come to the school and talk to the student. Then they typically go to the house and talk to the parents."

"So a phone call from you could get a child taken from the home?"

"No, it's a long road from suspicion of abuse to being removed from the home, and if it were to get to that level there needs to be a lot of evidence to warrant removal. If there is a problem, usually a visit from DHS is enough for parents to realize they need to handle things differently, and classes are offered for parents to learn different parenting techniques. There's a lot of interventions tried and rarely is a child removed from the home."

"So a kid can be a brat and the parent is trying their best and nothing happens to the kid?"

"I know a lot of people think that way, but if a parent chooses to get physical with their child and leaves a bruise that lasts more than 24 hours, then the parent needs to tone it down. I realize that being a parent is not easy, but getting excessively physical doesn't solve anything, and can often make the problem worse."

"I'm glad I don't have to do that kind of work," Hoot said.

"That's one of the harder parts of my job," I said. "What's some of the harder parts of your job, Hoot?"

"That's easy. Evicting tenants for not paying rent is tough, especially when there are kids involved."

"So that's just a different type of removal from the home, isn't it?"

He paused for a moment, then said, "I guess. I never thought of it that way. Just like you said, it takes a while to get to that point, but then the authorities get involved and all of their stuff gets put on the curb. It can get kind of ugly and I'm always glad a sheriff is around when push really does come to shove."

"We both work with people, just in very different ways, don't we?" I said.

"Right, but I'll take my job over yours any day."

"I think we both are in the right jobs," I said. "In the meantime I'm going to watch for kids doing unusual work that I can share with my students."

As we worked our way back toward Iowa we took the Ludington car ferry named the S.S. Badger across Lake Michigan to Manitowoc, WI which was quite an experience. "You should see how they pack in the cars and semis in the belly of this ship!" Hoot said.

"How did you get to see it?" I asked.

"Because they had me ride my motorcycle in, told me where to park, and then I had to strap it down. This ship is amazing!"

Losing sight of the shore on the four hour trip I swore I could see the curvature of the earth. Getting back onto dry ground we traveled a few hours back to Iowa, stopped at a roadside fruit stand and bought berries and peaches, then camped for the evening in Kendallville. The next day we rented kayaks to take a trip down the Upper Iowa river. This tributary of the Mississippi river, in the Driftless Area of northeast Iowa, was breathtaking.

"A good spot for a log cabin?" Hoot asked as we paddled along.

"Absolutely! This area is stunning!"

"Let's add it to the list," he said.

We were working our way down the river, enjoying the scenery when I asked something that was on my mind.

"So what was the story about your first marriage?" I asked.

"What do you want to know?"

"Whatever you want to tell me."

"Well, she was a good lady and had two kids. We'd been seeing each other for awhile and had talked about marriage but didn't have any concrete plans. At one point we went on a vacation in Mexico with some other couples. Evidently she had arranged for a justice of the peace to meet us on a beach. She told me that we were getting married that afternoon or we were done. I couldn't think of a good reason to not get married, so we did. It lasted a year until she found someone else. That's it in a nutshell."

"Ouch, I'm sorry. So there was no proposal, no ring, no engagement period, no big reception?"

"Nope, none of that. We each bought a few pieces of clothing from a nearby vendor for the ceremony. One of the other couples stood up as witnesses. We were already in Mexico so that became our honeymoon. I always figured I would get married once. I did that, and I burned that ticket. Until I met you I never considered getting married again."

"So is that where the 'no ultimatum' came from?

"I suppose so. I like that you're active, that you enjoy many of the same things I do, I'm surprised that you don't have kids, and we have similar dreams. That's all very attractive to me."

We let that conversation sit while we completed seven hours of paddling including the last two hours in steady rain, taking our time to see wildlife and amazing scenery. We got to the spot in Bluffton where the kayak company picked us up, and it finally had stopped raining by the time we returned to the campsite. Hoot left to find a warm meal for us while I showered and got into dry clothes. By the time he got back I had a nice fire going and a beach towel for a tablecloth on the picnic table.

"Nice fire! Did you have help?" he asked.

"No. I like to camp, remember? You're not the only one who can make a fire."

Putting the pulled pork sandwiches and coleslaw on the picnic table he drew me close and said, "that's something else I really appreciate about you."

"Can you be a bit more specific?"

"Adding on to what we said earlier, I like how you are independent and self-sufficient. You're low maintenance and don't ask for help unless you need it. I get tired of women who are always asking for my help when it's things they could do themselves."

"Thanks. Just remember that I might be low maintenance, but some maintenance is required."

"Message received," he said.

"By the way, remind me to show you a pair of pearl earrings I like in case some maintenance is ever needed."

"I'm happy to look at them, but I prefer things that are custom made, not things that are mass produced."

"I understand. While we're on the topic, something I appreciate about you is the care you take to consider things I might want to see and do, and though I don't think many people would describe you as 'tender', I do see that side of you."

"Don't tell anybody about the tender side of me, it would ruin my reputation."

"I promise. You have also exposed me to so many experiences that I would never have known about or would have considered. Like today. It never crossed my mind to go kayaking all day, but I had a great time! I love our summer trips!"

"I do too, and it helps that we like so many of the same activities. I could travel alone, but it's more enjoyable to share the experience. Thanks for making the scrapbook last year. It brings back so many memories. I see you're taking notes again on this trip."

"I enjoyed making the scrapbook as much as you enjoy looking at it, and yes, I plan to make a scrapbook of this trip, too."

We were planning to head straight home the next morning but we were close to Spillville, Iowa, where the collection of Bily clocks were housed. I had seen them before and knew Hoot would appreciate the craftsmanship involved. The Bily clocks were handmade masterpieces made by two bachelor farming brothers during the winter months. Henry Ford had offered the Bily brothers $1 million in 1928 for a clock. Even the Smithsonian museums were interested, but the brothers willed their clocks to the city of Spillville with the expectation that the collection would never be sold or divided. When I explained this to Hoot he said, "I don't want to go to a clock museum!" But this was one of the few times I insisted. He agreed as long as I paid the entrance fee.

Two hours later he paid me back the fee. "I've never seen anything like it! Thank you for making me stop!"

The real compliment came after we got back home and I overheard him telling his buddies about it. "You've got to check it out, it's incredible the work they did with woodworking and dentistry tools!"

When he noticed I was listening he had the grace to blush, and I returned his expression with a wink.

Chapter 5
Trip #3 - July 2002

We traveled 2,510 miles in 8 days on the Goldwing 1800. The numbers on the map represent where each day ended.	
1	Grand Forks, ND
2, 3, 4, 5	Flin Flon, Manitoba Province
6	Grand Rapids, Manitoba Province
7	Grand Forks, ND
8	Sioux City, IA (home)

Steve's parents were good friends with a married couple who lived in Flin Flon, Manitoba Province, Canada. They had invited Hoot to visit them sometime, so that was our summer destination. We weren't planning to camp on this trip, so we just used the saddle bags for our clothing and gear. The concept of packing light takes on an entirely different meaning when you only have one saddle bag for everything you need, leaving room for rain gear and the mandatory jar of crunchy peanut butter. The trip north was uneventful, but I was reminded of an important geography lesson.

"Steve, we've been riding for almost ten hours. Are we stopping in this little town for the night?"

"Well, it's supper time. How about getting a bite to eat and then go a bit farther? The more we ride today, the less we'll need to ride tomorrow."

"How much farther?"

"Let's ride until it gets dark," he suggested.

The current time was about 6:00 PM. I figured we would eat, stretch our legs and probably had about two more hours of riding ahead of us. I could handle that. Driving after dark in a wooded area can be risky in a car with animals darting out, or not seeing large roadkill, but it can be deadly on a motorcycle.

"Let's go!" I got back on the bike and looked forward to being done soon.

After two hours had passed the sun was still high in the sky. With a sinking feeling in my gut I realized my mistake. "We're going north, aren't we?"

"Yup," he said.

"The sun sets later in the north, doesn't it?"

"Yup," he said again, with a chuckle in his voice.

"And this is July so the sun probably sets really late, right?"

"Yup."

"So in your humble opinion, what time will the sun set tonight?"

"I'm guessing around 11:00."

That earned him a smack on his shoulders. We were in the middle of nowhere and we didn't have camping gear with us. The only choice was to keep riding.

"Last February," Hoot said, "when we took the snowmobile trip for your 40th birthday, you said you couldn't wait for our next motorcycle trip. So here we are on the Hooter Scooter and now you want off?"

"Last February I wasn't intending to spend over 12 hours on the bike in one day," I replied.

That birthday was significant in another way, too. While I had appreciated the opportunity to go snowmobiling, it wasn't what I had hoped for.

We had been cleaning up dinner dishes the weekend after my birthday and I was getting ready to go home to start the school week. I took a deep breath and said "Hoot, do you know how you've said to never give you an ultimatum?"

His raised eyebrows told me he was paying attention.

"Well, I'm not giving you one, but I gave myself one and my birthday was the deadline. You know I'd like to talk about marriage, but all you ever say is 'Let's talk about it later'. I know your past experience makes you hesitant about marriage, but we've been together for almost four years and I'm not going to wait anymore to have a serious conversation about it. We do talk about a log cabin but we're not doing anything about making it a reality. I appreciate everything you've done for me, the trips we've taken and the good times we've had. I love you, but I can't keep doing this. I'm done."

After a long pause Hoot asked, "What's his name?"

I wasn't sure what to expect from him but it never occurred to me that he would think there was someone else.

"There isn't anyone else, Hoot. There's only ever been you."

We finished up the dishes in silence, tears on our cheeks, and I gathered up the few things I had at his place. Driving home that evening was one of the most difficult things I'd done since I met him.

I couldn't sleep and was up early when I read an email from him the next morning.

"I couldn't sleep at all last night. I'm not mad at you, I'm mad at myself. I know I procrastinate, Mary. It was one of the hardest things I've done in four years to see you walk out of the door. I feel like I got kicked in the cojones. Please reconsider. I love you. I'll give you some space, and I promise to seriously think about marriage and to talk about it with you."

I wasn't ready to call him back. And though I was more than half finished with the quilt, I considered giving it to a quilting group to finish and donate.

Later that week the pair of pearl earrings I had admired showed up on my doorstep with a note from Hoot. 'I've hardly slept or eaten since last Sunday. I know I've taken you for granted. Please accept these earrings as an apology. It's been four days, please call me and let's talk.'

Deciding that everyone deserves a second chance I did finally call him. We met at a local restaurant for dinner. I wore the earrings. It was awkward at first, but we talked about a few things.

"I don't blame you for leaving," Hoot said. "I know we need to talk so I'll start. What are your thoughts about kids?"

"I like kids. I work with hundreds of them at school every day, but I'm 40 and getting too old to start having children. What do you think?"

"You need to know that kids are a deal breaker for me," he said. "I like my life the way it is, especially being able to pick up and go whenever I want, which is why I don't have a boss. Speaking of which, would you plan to keep teaching? It seems like you have a strict calendar every year."

"Yes, I worked hard to get my teaching license, I like what I do and I've supported myself for many years as a teacher. I haven't considered giving it up."

"I'd like to flip houses," Hoot said. "You could help with that. I'll do the manual labor, and you can do the decorating. You have a knack for making things look homey."

"Yes, I could do that, but I want to earn my own way. I like having my own money, the health insurance my job provides, and paying into a pension. I could still help with making things look homey."

"Seems like you're whoring yourself out for a job."

"I've never heard it put that way, but I'm paid a decent salary for what I do. I could probably get paid more if I worked outside of teaching, and I'm not opposed to doing something else, but I don't plan to stop teaching anytime soon. Besides, if we build a log cabin somewhere, I could probably find a teaching job nearby. I'm not tied to a location. And if we get married I wouldn't mind having a joint bank account. Two incomes are better than one, right?"

"No argument there, but what about church? If we got married would you expect me to become Catholic?"

"No. I don't expect you to do anything you're not comfortable with, but I would expect you to respect my choices."

"Good. I'm not comfortable in a church. I'm spiritual, just not religious. I can pray just fine in the woods or on the water. I don't need to be in a church to pray."

"Do you know the Lord's Prayer?"

"Is that the one that starts with 'Our Father'?"

"Yes."

"No, I've heard it, but I don't know it."

"That's the only thing I'd ask you to learn. It's a very common prayer and I would appreciate you learning it so you can join in when we are in settings where it would be used."

"I suppose I can do that. I've always wondered, do Catholics really drink wine from the same cup? I just can't imagine doing that with a bunch of people."

"Yes, we do, although it's not required. But you don't seem to have a problem passing around a funny looking cigarette with a bunch of guys you just met on a fishing trip."

"Well, that's true. So what about a dog?" Hoot asked. "They're great companions."

"I've only had farm dogs, but I'm OK with the idea of a mid sized dog. I don't want one so large that it's like a piece of furniture."

"I agree with that, and I'm glad we got some of that out in the open," Hoot said. "Is this the kind of thing you wanted to talk about?"

"Yes, for starters, but it bothers me that I had to walk out in order to have this conversation."

"I'll try to do better. If you have something on your mind just be blunt and tell me. I can handle it. What I can't handle is if you say something like, "If you really knew me you'd know what I'm thinking.'"

"I don't expect you to read my mind. That's why I always give you a list for Christmas gift ideas, but when I bring up anything about marriage your response is usually 'We'll talk about it later' then I'm not sure what I'm supposed to say."

"Yeah, I'll try to get better about that."

It wasn't long until we fell back into our routine. I kept working on the quilt and eventually we decided to make the trip to Canada.

So now we were back on the bike, headed to Flin Flon, Canada, no closer to marriage than we had been months earlier. There was nothing but open road in front of us and trees on the sides. It felt like a tree tunnel. The sun was starting to get a bit lower in the sky.

"How's that girl, Caprice doing?" he asked, breaking the silence of the road.

"She's a sophomore now, so I don't see her very often since she's at the senior high. She still stops by once in a while to say hi and she still wears oversized shirts. Evidently things are about the same at home."

"Do you have to call the authorities then?"

"I have to have reasonable suspicion of abuse. I think I've contacted DHS about Caprice at least ten times over the last few years but it always comes back unfounded."

"So then what do you do?"

"There's nothing more I can do. It's not up to me to decide what really happened."

"Seems like if they don't take action the first few times they're not ever going to take action. What a hassle for the parents."

"My responsibility is to the student. and I'm going to keep sending in reports whenever I have reasonable suspicion. I don't have any control on what happens after that."

We let the conversation sit for awhile and reality came back into focus as we rolled into one of the few gas stations on this route. It was about 9:00 PM and it was safer to fill up when we saw a gas station than take our chances later on. Fortunately we only had two hours left to ride.

"Welcome, Steve and Mary!" our new friends greeted us at the door of their cabin after we peeled ourselves off the bike. "Can we offer you anything to drink? I know 11:00 is a bit late, but I'm sure you're tired from traveling,"

"You have no idea!" I thought, but falling asleep to the call of loons helped to relieve tension from the hours in the saddle.

Flin Flon is an interesting place. Our host explained that the road ends there, so if you want to go further north you need a float plane. "Most people have a 4 wheel drive vehicle in the garage and a float plane on the lake," he said. "Including us, so we'll go up in the air and look around the area while you're here." I couldn't see Hoot's face, but I could sense a smile on his face after hearing about a plane ride.

"Mining is the primary industry, so the town is

built on rock," our host continued, "to the point that the homes in the old part of town were built around the rock which was exposed in the home."

"It must be hard to do any remodeling in those homes," Hoot said.

"Actually it was pretty easy. If you wanted more room in the house you chipped away at the rock and carried it out by the bucket load until you had the space you wanted!"

"I did that in my first apartment," our hostess explained. "It was very small with a lot of exposed rock. My roommate and I just kept chipping away at the rock, carrying it out in five-gallon buckets. Eventually our little apartment got bigger!"

"What is that?" I asked, pointing to what looked like an elevated wooden sidewalk.

"Those are sewer boxes," we were told. "One of the problems with building a town on top of rock is supplying water into the house and disposing of sewage out of the house, especially when the ground is frozen half the year. Years ago there was no water system so water was carried into the home and a bucket was used to carry raw waste out. Around 1930 they figured out a way to place sewer lines above ground and they are called 'sewer boxes.'"

"How do they work?" Hoot asked.

"A potable water supply line and a sewer line are piped inside a box with PVC piping. These are attached to the water system in the home. A third line is included for use in the winter when warm water is pumped to keep the other two lines working. Sawdust is used for insulation. It's a similar principle of a modern water and sewer system, only this is above ground.

"Sometimes I think I'm an old soul," Hoot said, "but I'll always be grateful for the modern sanitation system!"

We stayed in Flin Flon for a few days, fished for Northern Pike which they called jack fish, spent a lot of time on the water or in the air, and in general just saw the sights until we re-traced our steps back to Iowa. Another trip for the scrapbook.

Chapter 6
Birthday Surprise

We'd put many miles on the Hooter Scooter in the four years since our first date and found a few places that might qualify as log cabin territory. It was September and the quilt was almost done; it would be his Christmas gift.

"Are those steaks about ready, Birthday Boy?" I asked through a window overlooking his driveway in the summer of 2002.

"Almost," he replied, rolling his shoulders while checking the heat on the Big Green Egg.

"Tight shoulders?" I asked. "Feeling old now that you're almost 50?"

"No," he said "it feels like something is gripping my back."

"So when's the doctor appointment?" I asked, though I knew the answer. Steve often said, "Someday I'll probably have a health problem but I'll deal with it when it happens." By now it had been almost 15 years since seeing a doctor or dentist. I still expressed concerns about his health but he brushed them off, like he brushed off this back ache.

"I just need to do some stretches. I'll be OK," he said. "My back is messing me up right now. I had to break down and hire help to work on a roof this week.

I just can't be on a roof now. Maybe later."

"My roof is so steep I'm scared to get up on it because I'm not sure I could get down."

"You should take your phone with you, but generally speaking you women have it so easy, of course you could get down!"

"What do you mean by that?"

"If you're a woman and get stuck on a roof, or just get scared up there, all you have to do is start taking off your clothes and you'll have plenty of men there to help you. Some of them might even show up in a fire engine!"

"Oh brother. I should have figured you'd come up with that solution. What if a guy did that?"

"If a guy took off their clothes, a squad car would show up!"

"But back to the topic, when's the doctor appointment?" I asked again.

"I might need to find a doctor one of these days," he conceded, "but I'll wait until after my birthday."

His upcoming birthday marked six months since the time of my birthday when I said goodbye and walked out of his kitchen. Not much had changed after we got back together so instead of talking about it again, I decided to put it in writing, using old fashioned pen and paper.

"Steve, you told me to be blunt, and I don't want any assumptions, so I'm asking again that we talk about the possibility of having a future together. I love you. I don't want to push you into anything. I know you are hesitant. Sometimes I'm hesitant too. What are your concerns? One of my concerns is that we always have a good time when we're together, but in reality we don't see each other very often. During the majority of the year we only spend time together on the weekends. Our summer trips are great, but they're not the standard daily routine. Could we really live together, or are we both too independent to change the status quo? What do you think?" I left the letter on his kitchen table under the salt and pepper shakers.

"I got your letter," he said in an email. "Let's talk about it later."

By now it was about three weeks away from his 50th birthday. I had asked if I could throw him a party at Pop-N-Docs, the same place we went on our first date. Knowing neither of us liked surprises I wanted to make sure he was OK with it.

"That sounds like a lot of fun!" and he made a list of people he wanted to invite. I was touched that he wanted my mom to come too, and she was happy to be included.

"Mom, we're still not talking much about marriage," I told her a few days before the party. "I've tried to have conversations about our future and I get the feeling that he talks about it with some of his friends, but not with me. I think his first marriage makes him skittish, and I understand that, but if we can't even talk about having a future together, then what does that say for other important topics that come up?"

"So why have you stayed with him this long?" she asked.

"We have a good time when we're together, Mom.

He's smart, funny, and a hard worker. We enjoy a lot of the same things, and he respects other things that are important to me."

"So what are your concerns?"

"It feels like we're coming at this from very different angles. Just like our working environment; I'm used to working in a school system with structure, rules and process. He works within his own personal system doing what he wants, when he wants. Both of us do our weekday living in our own homes in our own way. Neither is right or wrong, but they are very different. We enjoy each other's company, but we can't seem to find that happy medium where we can meld our lifestyles together. I think the hitch is that he seems to focus on the big picture and I focus more on the details. The most time we spend together is on the weekends and on our summer trips. Those are big picture items. The finer details are day-to-day living. After so many years together I realize that we have very different ways of doing things, and since I'm 40 and he's turning 50 we're both pretty set in our ways. That's a big concern for me."

"So have you had that conversation?"

"I've tried. When I bring it up his typical response is 'we'll talk about it later', but later never comes. There's more to making a life together than a log cabin and summer vacations. I love him, and we've had a lot of good times but I can't keep doing this. I've come to accept that his silence is his answer. Once this party is over I'm done."

"Only you can decide what to do, honey," was her response.

The party went well with about 50 of his friends and family members at the marina, including plenty of motorcycles and boats, food and drink, cards and gifts. As the cake was being cut Hoot invited me to the front and I expected him to thank me for putting this gathering together. But that's not what happened.

Putting one arm around me, he raised the other arm to a friend on a raised deck nearby. On Hoot's cue a banner unrolled to read 'Mary, will you marry me?'

He slipped his arm down to hold my hand, then turned so he was facing me. I was aware everyone was whooping and hollering, but I stood frozen.

He was smiling. I'm not sure what my expression said. I felt like I was in shock. The letter I wrote him said that I was starting to question if marriage was a good idea. He said we would talk. This was his response? Just when I decided I was done, he wanted to get married? How did we get from 'let's talk about it later' to a proposal?

"Mary, say something," he prompted in a stage whisper.

I couldn't think. So many thoughts were intruding and I couldn't form a word. How did we start with a birthday party and end with a marriage proposal?

"Mary, say something," Hoot repeated as the clapping and hollering subsided and everyone was looking at me. I knew that only one word was acceptable here.

I wanted to say 'Could we go somewhere and talk about this?' But that wasn't an option.

"Mary, say something," Hoot was almost pleading.

"Yes," I said, which was the only appropriate thing to say. The clapping and hollering started up again.

"Is there a ring to go along with this?" I asked, wondering how far he had planned this occasion.

"No, I thought you would want to help pick it out or get one custom made," he said.

After a round of hugs, kisses and good wishes Hoot wanted to show me the banner. It was professionally made in rip-proof vinyl and was anchored to hang straight using a few bolts, one of which fit my finger just right so I wore it for the evening.

"What a woman!" Hoot said, "Wearing a bolt for a ring!"

"Did you have a date in mind?" I asked Hoot as the party continued with boat rides and more food and drink.

"No, there's plenty of time to talk about that." For once I found myself grateful for that time to decide what to do, and I wondered what the motivation was behind the proposal? Did he really want to be married?

Getting a few moments alone with my mom she said that Hoot had asked her just before the party if she would give her blessing to our marriage. Mom had said, "Are you sure?" and Steve had said "Mary and I have talked about it a lot and I'm going to ask her tonight."

"Steve is a nice guy," Mom said, "and I wasn't going to get in the way, but I wasn't sure where things stood between the two of you so I gave him my approval."

"I don't know what I'm going to do, Mom. I wouldn't say we've talked about it a lot. I feel like I have to force him into talking about it. That's not the way this should work. He knows how I feel and his silence has given me his answer. Until now."

The next day Hoot gave me a list of people he wanted at the wedding, and mentioned that he was looking at Barefoot Cruises for the honeymoon. He had obviously been thinking about this, but marriage is more than a proposal or a ceremony. I was tempted to just walk away but I knew that his decision to propose had not been made lightly, and after saying yes to his proposal I felt an obligation to him, and to us, to get this all out in the open. Initially I had wanted to get married and he was hesitant. Now, when I was expressing hesitancy he had proposed.

We really needed to talk, but soon something else added another layer to the situation.

Chapter 7
Caprice

A few weeks after the birthday party I got a phone call from the high school counselor. "Mary, can you come over? A student is in my office. She won't talk to me, but said she would talk to you. This is serious. How soon can you be here?" After a few specific questions I understood this was regarding the student I called Caprice.

Getting someone to cover my class I went to the senior high and walked into the guidance area. The high school counselor met me and explained what was happening with Caprice. "They are doing a swim unit in PE. Evidently Caprice usually wears a T-shirt over her suit, but the swim coach saw her without her T-shirt on and there's bruises all over her back. The coach had her get dressed and brought her to my office. The school nurse looked at her back and also noticed more bruising on the underside of her arms, like you would see if someone were protecting their face. Caprice won't talk to me and said she would only talk to you. I'll let the two of you alone, but I've already called the police and DHS. I'm not going to let her go home tonight."

Walking into his office Caprice was sitting with the school nurse. With permission from Caprice, the nurse showed me the bruises, covered Caprice in a blanket and left the two of us alone.

"Did Dad do that to you?" I asked.

She nodded. She was shaking and her legs were bouncing.

"So all the times I asked about bruises and you said they were from softball, what was the actual truth?"

"I lied. Once in a while they were from softball but the bad ones were from dad. When he drinks he gets mean and he takes it out on me. When you would ask me about it I didn't know what would happen if I told the truth, so I lied. I'm just so tired of covering it up, and I purposely didn't pull down my T-shirt in time when the swim coach looked my way. I wanted someone to see this. I'm tired of being scared every time I go home."

"Can I give you a hug?" I asked, aware that I didn't want to make physical contact if she didn't want it.

"Yes!" she said, turning her face into my shoulder and sobbing. I put my arms around her and cried too, imagining how much pain she endured to inflict the bruises that I saw.

"What's going to happen to me now?" she asked, her voice muffled in my shoulder.

"The authorities are on their way, and they will talk to you. Tell them the truth and don't try to protect your dad. Someone will talk to your dad after they talk to you. You will not be allowed to go home tonight. Is there anyone you can stay with for a few days while this gets worked out?"

I asked the question as a matter of protocol, but I knew the answer. Caprice had told me she didn't have any family in the area. In this rural area of Iowa there weren't extra beds available either. I wasn't sure what was going to happen.

"Will you stay with me for awhile?" Caprice asked.

"I'll stay as long as you need me," I said.

Soon the police and DHS showed up and the small guidance office was packed, so we moved to a nearby conference room. Students and staff were startled to see so many official looking people walking down the hall, surrounding Caprice who was walking close to me.

After Caprice explained what had been happening the police left to talk to her dad. The DHS representative asked Caprice where she could stay. There were no options forthcoming, and I knew the likely possibility was to give her a bed at a juvenile delinquent center in a nearby large town. That was not a good option so taking a deep breath I spoke up. "I know Caprice and I haven't talked about this, and I'm not a licensed foster care site, but I have a spare room at my home and Caprice could stay with me. Would that be OK?"

"I'm OK with that," the DHS rep said. "Since you've already cleared background checks through the school there would be no problem on my end, although we wouldn't be able to help with expenses since you're not officially a foster care parent. Caprice, would that be OK with you?"

"Yes!" she said, almost jumping in my lap.

"Expenses are not a problem," I said. Turning to Caprice I said, "You will be allowed to go to your home to get some things. Bring them back to school and put them in your locker or in your counselor's office. I'll see you after school."

After she left to get her personal items, I headed back to my office and the thought struck me that I wasn't sure how Hoot was going to respond to this. I usually called him on my way home during my 30 mile drive, but that routine was going to change starting today. I sent him an email and said, "Unusual day. I won't be able to call on my way home, but I'll give you a call tonight and explain."

A duffel bag appeared in my office over the lunch period, and Caprice showed up after school.

"Am I really going home with you?" she asked.

"Yes. I live alone and have plenty of room. You can stay as long as you need." I knew I was doing the right thing, but I had no idea how Hoot was going to respond to this.

"Aren't you married?"

It occurred to me that I knew a lot about her but she didn't know much about me so I filled her in on the basics as we walked to the staff parking lot. 'Not married but have a significant other with the nickname of Hoot. Like animals but have no pets. Grew up on a farm. Enjoy being outside, camping, traveling, music. Like to bake. Enjoy reading and writing.' She took it all in but by the time we got to the car she was unusually quiet. I think reality was starting to set in for her.

"You can pick a radio station if you'd like," I said, breaking the silence.

"OK, how about something local?" and she found a station playing Lee Greenwood's hit "I'm Proud to be an American," and we both sang along with easy listening country music for the next 30 minutes until I pulled up to my yellow split level home.

"Is my dad going to find me here?" Caprice wanted to know as I backed into the garage.

"No. I'm not sure how it works, but he will not be told you are with me. I assume he's been told that you are safe. And even if he found out, he wouldn't know how to contact me."

"Couldn't he call school and ask?"

"He can call and ask, but they won't tell him. Just like you can't call a doctor's office and ask for the personal phone number and home address of your doctor because that is private information. Besides, I don't know your dad, but if he showed up here all it would take is one phone call from me to the police and he would be in even more trouble. You are safe here."

We spent some time getting her settled in her room, then went to the store since I needed some groceries. The only thing she added to the cart was orange juice. After returning home we made spaghetti with meat sauce for dinner and I put a loaf of banana bread in the oven for breakfast the next morning.

"Do you have homework to do?" I asked after the dishes were done and the bread was cooling.

"Yes, but not much," she said.

While she did her homework upstairs, I went downstairs and called Hoot.

"Interesting day?" he asked.

"Do you remember the girl that I've said is often on my mind?"

"Caprice?" he asked

"Right. Well, she's upstairs doing her homework right now."

"Whaaat?"

"Do you remember when I told you it's highly unusual for a student to be removed from the home?"

"Right, like it takes a long time to get to the point of evicting a tenant."

"Right. Well, she's got a lot of deep, fresh bruises that were noticed by a teacher. She admitted that dad caused them. Police and DHS were called. She's not allowed to go home while DHS does their investigation and I offered to let her stay with me since there aren't any available foster homes around here.

"That seems like a good thing," Hoot said. "How long is she going to be there?"

"I don't know, but I assume at least a few days."

"Do you think she would like a ride on the Hooter Scooter?"

"I think she would like that, but let's see how this goes. I'm not sure what to expect."

Heading back upstairs I found that Caprice was stuck on a history study guide.

"Can you help me?" she asked.

"Sure!" I said with more confidence than I felt, but how difficult could a sophomore study guide be? After looking at the study guide and her book for a moment I said, "Do you notice a pattern?"

"What do you mean?"

"The questions and their answers go in the same order as the pages in the book."

She paused and checked to see if my comment was accurate. It was.

"What! I never knew that!"

Finishing up her homework she wanted to take a shower and then was ready for bed.

"What time do we leave in the morning?" she wanted to know.

"Later than you're used to," I said, standing at the door of the guest room. "I leave the house at 7:30 so I'm at school by 8:00. Do you want me to wake you up?"

"Yes, could you wake me up at around 7:00?"

"You bet." After a pause I said, "Can I sit on your bed and just talk for a bit?"

She nodded.

"You've had a tough day," I said as I sat on the bed and she leaned up on the pillow. "How are you now? Do you have questions for me?"

"Well it was crazy when the police took me home. They let me run in for about 10 minutes and grab some clothes. I'm not even sure what I took."

"I can make arrangements for you to go back home and get more clothes if needed, or we can take the opportunity to go shopping, too."

"OK, thanks. What do you think is happening with my dad?"

"I have no idea. My priority is you. I imagine the police have talked to him and he's allowed to be at his home tonight. He'll probably have more conversations about everything tomorrow."

"I don't get it. He did something wrong, but he gets to stay and I have to leave. That seems twisted."

"I can't argue with your thinking, but would you want to stay home alone?"

"Not really, but I didn't do anything wrong, did I?"

"No. And even if you did something wrong, your dad is an adult and cannot treat you the way he did."

It was quiet for a few moments and then she asked,

"What's going to happen in the morning?"

"I usually get up around 5:00 and go to the gym, but I don't want to leave you here alone so I'll skip the gym and get up around 6:00. I'll have coffee and read the paper and get ready for school before I wake you at 7:00. Then we'll have a bite to eat and leave for school. Does that sound ok?"

She nodded, then asked, "What's going to happen to me? Can you adopt me?"

"I don't know how the process works. This will probably be temporary, and then you will go back home with your dad, or possibly live with some relatives. Adoption would mean that your dad would sign away his parental rights. I understand that you and your dad have some problems, but I don't think he would sign away his rights to you."

"If I live somewhere else then I would have to go to a different school, right?"

"It depends where you live, but yes, it often involves going to a different school."

It was silent for a few beats, then she asked, "If I stay here for awhile, could you teach me how to do laundry? And maybe how to bake things like banana bread?"

"Sure! But I happen to know for certain that you took a family and consumer science class where laundry and quick breads were taught, right?"

"Well, yes, I was in the class, but I was busy checking out the guys and didn't pay attention to the teacher."

"Gotcha. Yes, I'll be happy to teach you those things without any distractions."

Caprice nodded, then yawned. Her eyes were

getting heavy.

"I know you're a teenager, but would you like to get tucked in?"

Her eyes got shiny. "Yes," she whispered.

Tucking her into bed I turned off the light and asked, "Door open or shut?"

"I sleep with it shut at home, but could we leave it open tonight? And maybe leave the bathroom light on?"

"Of course. You're safe here, sleep well, but I'm right next door if you need me."

The night passed without incident and I woke her at 7:00 the next morning.

"How did you sleep?" I asked.

"Great! But I have a question for you."

"What's that?"

"What do I call you? At school I call you Ms. Snyder, but that seems weird if I'm staying here."

"I'm ok with whatever you're comfortable with. You can call me Mary when we're here, but you'll probably be more comfortable calling me Ms. Snyder at school. Besides, you're not at my school anymore so it's not like you'll see me in the hallways."

"OK. Can I have banana bread and orange juice for breakfast?"

"You bet."

"You'd make a great mom, Mary. I think you should adopt me."

"You have a parent, Caprice, but thanks for the vote of confidence."

The next few days followed a similar pattern. We always had music playing and she became more relaxed. I suspected I was filling a maternal place in her world, and realized she was filling a daughter's space in mine.

"So how's it going?" Hoot asked, "And how long is Caprice going to stay with you? Should I take you two out to dinner or something?"

"It was a little awkward at first, but it's becoming more comfortable. Evidently she's telling all the kids at school that she's staying at my house and according to Caprice they all think I'm strict and no nonsense so they're having a hard time believing her when she tells them I like to garden and bake and do homey kinds of things. The other day she wanted to bake banana bread in the morning so it was still warm when we left for school. She took it along to share with her friends, and I'm told some of her friends are jealous and want to live here too.

"I hope you put your foot down on that!"

"I thought it was funny, but I made it clear that they had their own homes."

"So what's the plan?"

"I'm in frequent contact with the DHS people. It doesn't sound like Caprice will be going back home anytime soon. They are looking for a long term foster home but there's not many places available, especially not ones that will allow Caprice to stay in the same school."

"What do you mean? Why would she need to go to a different school?"

"Because your address determines the school district you attend."

"OK, but she's living with you 30 miles from her school, but still going to the same place."

"Right, but this is temporary, and I work in the

school district she's attending. Those are different circumstances."

"This is temporary, right?"

"I assume so. The only other option right now would be a bed in the juvenile detention center, but I know DHS is looking for a family to take Caprice in."

"What's going on with her dad?"

"I don't know, but evidently it must be serious because this is turning into a longer stay which tells me there are some larger issues."

Saturday arrived and Hoot came over on the Hooter Scooter. Introducing the two of them, Hoot surprised both of us when he gave Caprice a beautiful long stemmed rose. "I'm sorry to hear about what's going on with your dad, but I want you to know there's still a lot of good men out there."

"And he is a good one," I thought.

After putting the rose in a vase, Caprice started asking Hoot questions about the bike.

"Would you like to go for a ride?" he asked.

Her eyes lit up like a little kid on Christmas morning, so I got her bundled up and they left for about 30 minutes. She was still grinning when they returned. "That was great!" she said.

"I'm going to run a few errands and then can I take you two ladies out to lunch?" Hoot asked.

"Sure! Should we meet you somewhere?"

"There's that cantina that we like, how about going there?"

"Caprice, are you OK with Mexican food?"

"Yes!"

Hoot left to run some errands and Caprice had nonstop questions for me about Hoot. "You've been dating for almost five years and you're not married?" she asked.

"Well, actually, he just proposed recently," I said.

"Where's your ring?" she asked.

"We haven't gotten that far," I said.

About an hour later we were having chips and salsa while waiting for our meals. Caprice was busy asking questions about motorcycles and our trips. Then out of the blue she asked, "Hey Hoot, why doesn't Mary have a ring yet? Aren't you supposed to give her a ring when you propose?"

It was such an innocent question, but it hung in the space between us, and the air felt heavy.

"We're getting there," Hoot finally replied. I was grateful that Caprice kept up her questions about Hoot's work and his motorcycle, unaware of the change in atmosphere her question created.

On our way home from the restaurant Caprice and I talked about plans for the next morning.

"Do you attend a particular church?" I asked her. "I can go with you to a church if you'd like, or would you want to come with me?"

"I've never gone to church but I'd like to check it out. Can I go with you?"

"Sure, but I play piano so I sit in the front facing a lot of people. You can sit right beside me and turn pages for me, or sit in a pew nearby."

"Do I have to decide now?"

"No, I just want you to know your options."

After Caprice was in bed that evening I called Hoot to thank him for treating Caprice so well and for buying lunch.

"Did you tell her to ask about the ring?" he asked.

"No, I did not. She was full of questions about you and asked why we weren't married yet. I told her you had proposed, and she asked to see my ring. I told her we hadn't gotten that far yet."

It was quiet for a few beats and then Hoot asked, "Where are things with you and Caprice? What you're doing for her is admirable, but all your time is spent with her. I don't even see you at the gym in the mornings. Our conversations are short and all about her. I get it, but I keep remembering that she's asked you to adopt her. Are you considering that?"

"She's only been here about a week, Hoot. I don't know what to think. Right now it's a lot of fun and she's easy to have around. She and I both took a chance because we only knew each other from school and we could have both been very different. So far so good."

"OK, but what about adopting her? You know I don't want kids. A teenage girl is not part of this package."

"Adoption is not even on the table. Just like it's a long process to be removed from the home, it's a long time to get to a point of adoption. I've been in contact with DHS and they've said they will need to get her placed with a certified foster home so she can't stay here forever."

"I miss you. I miss the time we spend together. She's a nice kid, but she's a kid. "

"I miss you too but we'll get this figured out."

"I hope so," Hoot said.

The next morning we went to a Catholic service and Caprice sat right beside me on the piano bench. I was surprised she wanted to do that because it can be intimidating to look out at a sea of faces, but it didn't seem to faze her.

"That was cool!" she said on the way home. "Do you do that every weekend?"

"Most weekends, yes."

"Do you play for different churches?" she asked.

"I play for different Catholic churches around town," I replied.

"Aren't there different kinds of churches?"

"Yes. There are many different Christian churches, but the basics are pretty much the same."

We enjoyed Sunday afternoon doing yard work and baking. She did some schoolwork and it all felt very normal, but a phone call the next day changed the routine.

"We have a foster home lined up for Caprice," the DHS social worker said. "It won't be immediate, but in a few days she should be in a different home."

Telling Caprice was tough, but I was surprised by her response. "I like being here with you Mary, but I've never had a brother or sister, so I hope that's the kind of place where I'm going. Do you know anything about this family?"

"Nothing. All I know is what the social worker told me, which is what I told you."

Telling Hoot created a different reaction. "I'm glad you provided a home for her, Mary, but I'd be lying if I didn't say I'm glad things between us will get back to normal."

Lying in bed later I was overwhelmed with emotions. Although adoption wasn't on the table, long term foster care could be a possibility assuming I would be approved. Was I prepared to have a teenage girl live with me, and have my life turned upside down? Her life was already turned upside down, how selfish was it of me to be able to help but not want to upset my life? I couldn't provide her what I knew she wanted, which was a nuclear family with siblings. What about Hoot? We didn't have concrete plans, or did we? He had proposed but it felt like he had popped the question so I wouldn't leave again. Or not? Did he really want to get married? Did I? I didn't sleep well the rest of the week.

On her last morning in my home Caprice and I made plenty of banana bread to take with her to her new family. It was quiet on the ride to school with her duffel bag in the backseat. The ride home was even quieter.

"So she's gone?" Hoot asked that night.

"Yes. She was with me for almost two weeks but she's with her new family tonight."

"She's a nice kid in a tough situation. I hope it works out for her."

"I do too." Caprice was gone from my home but never far from my thoughts. I had decided not to pursue being a foster parent, but I attended her home softball games and saw her occasionally at school when she would stop by to say hi. I asked how she was doing in her foster home, but she was non-committal. A few weeks after leaving my home she admitted that it wasn't working out with this family so she was getting moved to another home outside of the school district. It didn't sound like she was going to return home to live with dad. She was leaving in a few days and then we wouldn't see each other anymore. I went home and made a care package including orange juice and banana bread. I had no way to stay in touch with her since she didn't have a personal computer and student emails on school computers were strictly for communicating with school personnel. Social media hadn't been created yet. I would need to send letters to DHS and they would forward them to wherever Caprice was living. It wasn't great, but it was the best arrangement possible under the circumstances. I gave her a big hug goodbye and promised to write.

Chapter 8
Changes

By now it was fall 2002 and it had been almost six weeks since the birthday party surprise proposal. I was aware that I wasn't excited about the wedding or the marriage. It felt like I was going through the motions. Was this the 'cold feet' people talked about? I had already walked away once. If I walked away again I needed to be absolutely sure. I didn't know how to talk about it with Hoot, but this time he was the one to bring it up. He called one evening around dinner time and asked if I was home because he wanted to come over. He didn't come in but stood at the door. He seemed determined, like there was something on his mind that he needed to get off his chest. It was a side of him I didn't see very often.

"Mary, I feel like you don't want to get married anymore. There's a distance between us and I feel like you've changed your mind about being together. Am I right?"

Taking a deep breath I said, "I love you, Hoot, but I'm not sure I can see us spending our lives together. Do you?"

"I gave you what you wanted by asking you to marry me. Do you have any idea how much I thought about it before I asked you? Did you change your mind?"

"What I wanted? Isn't it what you want, too? I have no idea how much you thought about it because you didn't share those thoughts with me. I thought I wanted to get married, Hoot, but like I put in the letter I left on your table, we only spend time together on the weekends and in the summer. Otherwise we talk on my way home from school. What about the everyday ordinary routine? Neither of us are young and we are both pretty set in our ways. Could we live together day in and day out? For a long time I thought it could work but I'm not so sure anymore. Being with you seems so natural, but talking about marriage seems so forced. I love you, but yes, I've changed my mind about marriage."

After a long pause, his eyes tearing up, Hoot said, "I hope you never hurt another man like you've just hurt me," and he walked back to his truck.

I couldn't breathe. I had to get away. This wasn't the conversation with him that I had envisioned. Ten minutes later I had thrown some clothes in a bag and took off driving through tears while reliving the last few years, three amazing trips and so many great memories. I stopped driving when I was exhausted and found a motel room in a town called Harlan 100 miles away. I knew I wouldn't be able to sleep at home, but I couldn't sleep in Harlan, either. I kept seeing Hoot crying at my door. I ached for how much I missed him, but I still couldn't see us married. It just wasn't working.

I called in sick the next day and worked my way

back home. Walking around my home, feeling lost, I checked my email. There was a note from Hoot.

"Mary, I can't sleep. I don't know what happened to us. I miss you."

"Steve," I replied, "you told me you thought a lot before the proposal. I had thought a lot too. I wish we could have shared these thoughts with each other. In the past six months since breaking up and getting back together we still didn't get much out in the open about having a future together, so I had decided that after your birthday party I was going to say goodbye. Then when you proposed out of the blue, in front of so many people I wanted to ask if we could go talk about it somewhere, but that wasn't an option. I didn't have a choice except to say yes. Saying anything else would have been so embarrassing for both of us. We've both talked about not liking surprises, so a marriage proposal was a hell of a surprise. But just because we don't say 'I do' doesn't mean we have to say goodbye."

For the next few weeks it was easier to communicate through email than on the phone or in person as we tried to talk and sort out how to salvage our friendship.

While doing yard work on a warm late autumn day I saw Hoot ride by on the Hooter Scooter. I recognized his shirt as one he wore on special occasions. I waved. He stopped and we had an awkward conversation about 'how have you been, what's been going on,' and I asked about his back problems.

"Have you been to see a doctor yet?"

"No, I need to make an appointment one of these

days."

"No matter what, Hoot, I care about you. Would you please let me know what you find out?"

"Yeah, I can do that."

"I'm surprised to see you in my neighborhood. Special occasion?" I wondered if he had come across town to take a chance on seeing me, but that wasn't his style.

"After we broke up one of my friends took me to a speed dating event, and I met somebody who lives a few blocks away from here."

I could feel my eyes tear up. It really was over.

"Well, I hope you have a good time."

"Mary, nothing can take away our time together. We have gone on some great trips, had some amazing experiences and those good memories will always be there."

"Agreed." Feeling the tears well up I said "I need to finish up with the yard Hoot, but please stay in touch and let me know how your doctor appointment goes. I care about you."

"Will do," he said as he rode away.

Our emails and phone conversations went in phases. Sometimes we were in frequent contact, other times we went through dry spells. But finally came the news I had been waiting to hear.

Chapter 9
PSA

❝I promised that I would tell you news about my health," Hoot's voice message said. "Give me a call sometime."

"So what's the news?" I asked when I called that evening. It was around Thanksgiving, 2002.

"The pain in my back was getting worse and nothing I did was making it feel better, so I went to the community clinic. X-rays look fine, but they did blood work. I had to wait a few days for the results and then they called saying they want me back."

"Because why?"

"They said the back pain was probably caused by either gallbladder problems because gallbladder issues can radiate to the upper back, or prostate cancer. Either way they want to see me again."

I felt an internal switch labeled 'life changing event' flip inside me. "Why do they think cancer?" I asked.

"Before I answer that, tell me what you know about PSA's."

"Public service announcements? What does that have to do with anything?"

"No, goofball," I could almost see him rolling his eyes over the phone. "PSA means prostate specific antigen. It's a guy's hormone."

"OK," I said. "So why do they think it might be cancer?"

"A normal PSA number is around 4 or lower. Anything above 4 is a concern. Evidently my number is 76."

My proverbial internal switch had started glowing red. The man I still loved was obviously very ill.

"So have you gone back yet?"

"No," he continued, "And I'm not going to go back. Their test is wrong."

"Hoot," I said, "What do you mean you're not going back? This is serious!"

"I'm overweight, I eat too many fried pork rinds and don't exercise, unless you count all the times I beat your ass in racquetball. I just need to take better care of myself. If I'm not careful the pork plant will catch me and load me in the truck because bacon prices are up right now. Besides, I don't have any symptoms of prostate cancer. Their test is wrong. I've got things I need to do and I don't have time to keep going to the doctor. I'll deal with it later."

Checking online I realized he did have indications of prostate cancer; I wasn't sure if he had blood in the urine, but I had noticed his frequent urination, interruptions of the urine stream and inability to maintain an erection over the past few years.

"I'm fine," he would say when I expressed concern. "No problems."

One positive that came out of this problem was that Hoot and I were talking more. I think he was scared though he didn't admit that. But he knew I cared and I knew, pretty much, about his attitude toward the medical field and life in general.

One Sunday morning just before Christmas 2002, I was playing some prelude music at church and saw Hoot sitting in my direct line of sight. I'm sure I looked surprised, but I smiled and nodded his way. He nodded back. Other than our summer trips he had never attended a service with me and I was stunned to see him. After the service I noticed that he was not only waiting for me, but was visiting with a small group of people that seemed to know him.

"Hi," I said when he was free.

"Hi," he replied. "I've never heard you play at church so I decided to come. I hope it's OK."

"You're always welcome," I said.

"I don't go to church very often so I don't know what the music is supposed to sound like, but it seems like you do a good job."

"Thanks, I enjoy it."

"I had no idea I knew so many people at this church. It confirms what I've always thought, that there's a lot of hypocrites at church."

"Maybe us hypocrites are at church because we know we need help."

Pausing for a moment he nodded and said, "I suppose. I never thought of it that way. Anyway, do you think we could go out for coffee and just talk?"

I had to play at another service in an hour so we agreed to go out to lunch that day. Since it was almost Christmas I decided to give him the quilt. I had bought the fabric with him in mind, and I made it for him, so I decided he should have it rather than donating it somewhere.

"It's beautiful!" he said later that day, unfolding it

and running his hands over the rag quilt seams. "Is this the fabric you bought on our first trip that I could feel in the trailer?"

"One and the same. It took me a while, but I think it turned out really well."

"It feels awkward to not have a gift for you, but I do appreciate this and I'll use it."

Despite the change in our relationship, we ended up having a pleasant lunch and talked about our trips, grateful that we took them when we did. Hoot didn't want to talk about his health, other than saying that he didn't believe the results of the numerous medical tests that had been run.

Not a fan of doctors or their fees, Hoot tried numerous self help options for the next few months. Friends and family pleaded with him to return to the doctor but he was adamant that he could heal himself. He started an exercise regime, bought a juicer, and grew wheat grass to make his own healthy smoothies, threw out the fried pork rinds and added more fruits and vegetables into his diet, saw his chiropractor (who encouraged him to see his family doctor), and increased his use of cannabis which dulled the pain but didn't address the cause. The only difference any of this made was to stall treatment. He finally admitted he needed help and in early 2003 he agreed to have his gallbladder removed. That didn't solve the problem either. By then his PSA was well over 100.

I stopped by to see him after his gallbladder surgery. "That was pointless," Hoot said, while opening a medical bill and tossing it on a pile of similar looking bills. "The only guy helped by this surgery was the doctor. I still hurt. Do you know those assholes are charging me for the anesthesiologist, and the surgeon, and the doctor visits? I'm getting multiple bills. Just when I think I've got the last bill I get another one in the mail. And it didn't work! I still hurt!"

"They're concerned about the PSA number, right?" I asked, tiptoeing around a sensitive subject.

"Yeah, they're concerned, but I'm not. I don't have cancer. And I'm not paying the bills for the gallbladder surgery, either! When you hired me to fix your air conditioner you wouldn't have paid me until the problem was fixed. My gallbladder was not the problem and I didn't need the surgery. This sick care system is messed up, and I'm not paying them!"

"You mean the health care system?"

"No, they don't care about health. They make money when I'm sick. It's a sick care system and I'm not paying them!"

"Good luck with that," I said. "And for the record, I think I'm still paying for the air conditioner!"

"For the record," he replied, his tone softening, "you're the best return on $7 I ever made! If we would have gotten married then I would be on your insurance, but even without insurance I need to figure out what's going on with my health."

It took a moment to let his comment sink in. "That's why you wanted to get married? So you'd be on my insurance?"

"No! But insurance would have been a nice benefit. Then I could have seen a doctor and dentist and get some things addressed with my health. I know I'm changing the subject here but I've been wondering, have you ever heard anything about Caprice?"

"I did initially because she was still in the same school system and she would stop by once in a while, but then she was moved to a different family and a different school. I sent her a lot of letters and birthday gifts through the DHS office but I've never heard back. I'm not sure what's going on. It's possible the letters were never forwarded, or they were forwarded but the foster parents didn't give them to her, or she received the letters but never replied."

"So what happened with her dad? She never moved back home? Did she get adopted?"

"I don't know what happened with her dad. I think she is in long term foster care, not adopted. From what I understand, long term foster care usually happens when the parent doesn't fix things on their end, like if they were ordered to go to therapy or some kind of class but they refused to go, or they didn't complete treatment. The parents keep their parental rights, but the child isn't allowed to live with them."

"I'm curious. Keep me posted, OK?"

"Sure, I can do that," I said.

"By the way, I made you something," he said, handing me a bag. "I hope you like them."

Opening the bag I pulled out a few wooden items. "These are gorgeous, Hoot!"

"Do you know what they are?" he asked.

"They're trivets!" I said as I pulled out various sizes of square lattice items. Two were approximately 8x8, another two were approximately 4x4, all about one inch high. Knowing he had numerous wood working tools in his shop I asked how he had made it.

The part I understood was that each of them were made out of one piece of wood. The part I didn't understand was how he had made something so intricate all in one piece.

"Thank you, Hoot," I said, giving him a hug.

"You're welcome," he said, hugging me back and tickling my ribs.

I flinched.

"I still got it!" he said.

Chapter 10
Trip #4 - Spring 2003

We traveled 1,370 miles in about 24 hours in a Ford F150 long box (4 wheels!) on our trip south.	
1, 2, 3, 4, 5, 6	Mercedes, TX
7	Sioux City, IA (home)

Hoot's parents spent winter months in a mobile home retirement park in Mercedes, Texas. Hoot wanted to visit them, and he called me one day.

"You and I have always traveled well, and you get along with my parents. What do you think about going to visit them in Texas this spring?"

I took a few days off of school and we packed up his Ford F150 extended cab long box truck and off we went. Enough time had passed from the tension of the previous year that the conversation was comfortable, and since I was able to help drive we drove straight through with stops in San Antonio and Corpus Christi. Just 24 hours after leaving Iowa we were saying hello to his parents. While there we went to the local farmer's market which was so large it could have been a day long experience. It was my first experience with jicama and other foods from the area.

We walked into Progreso, Mexico, one day and did some shopping although I felt guilty carrying purchases in my arms while so many children were begging for a few coins. Every evening we enjoyed a meal at a local restaurant with fresh seafood followed by a swim at the park pool. What a nice change of pace from the snow and cold of Iowa.

I learned a lot about Hoot during my long visit with his parents.

"Did Steve tell you about flying his plane under the river bridges?" his dad asked.

"Or under the overpasses on the interstate?" his mom added.

Steve laughed as he recounted one day in particular.

"It was a beautiful day for flying, and I could see for miles. There was a stretch of interstate below me and no cars in sight. I wanted to try a touch and go on the interstate so I decided to go under an overpass. What I didn't know is that a cop was parked under there! I touched down, went right beside the cop who looked like he was sleeping, then pulled back into the air. I turned to see if the cop came out. I must have set off his radar. Wow, he came flying out with his lights flashing but there wasn't a car in sight! I laughed so hard I almost peed my pants!"

"Steve has liked anything that moved ever since he was little," his dad said. "Once he got on a motorcycle we never got him off. How many do you own now, Steve?"

"Only two, Dad," Steve replied, "my 2000 Honda Goldwing and 2001 Harley Road King, but I might get another one soon."

"What would you do with another one?" his dad asked.

"A smaller bike for running errands around town. It would be cheaper to run than my truck."

"Right, Ford F150's are great for hauling and towing, but expensive to use for a trip to the grocery store. How many boats do you have?"

"None right now. The problem with boats is that you use them the same season you ride motorcycles so I need to decide if it's going to be another motorcycle or a small boat.

"On that theory you can only ride one motorcycle at a time, right?" his dad said.

"Yes, but different bikes have different purposes. The Wing is a touring bike, I use that for long trips like what Mary and I have done. I use the Harley for shorter trips," Hoot explained.

"How about your plane?" His dad asked.

"I sold my Piper and let my license expire. But Mary paid for me to have an hour in the air for my birthday a few years ago. I had to go with an instructor but it was like riding a bike. What a great feeling to be back in the air again!"

On Sunday we found a Catholic church called the Basilica of Our Lady of San Juan Del Valle National Shrine. Although most of it was in Spanish, which I don't speak, the mariachi band kept my toes tapping most of the service! Another day was spent at South Padre island and we caught a kite festival and contest in full swing. The sky was colorful with kites which we could appreciate from our own kite flying experiences, but I hadn't heard of kite contests.

"How can you have a kite flying contest?" I asked Hoot. "How do you win?"

"It's like gymnastics where you maneuver your kite to do stunts. There's also something called kite fighting, have you ever heard of it?"

"No, how do you fight with a kite?"

"They use a special type of sharp thread instead of kite string, and the goal is to maneuver your kite to cut the other guys' kite thread before they cut yours," Hoot explained. "Last kite in the air wins!"

On one of the last nights there I went to the community center and watched Hoot and his dad play in a pool tournament. These guys were serious about playing pool! Toward the end of each game they created a rule about what had to happen before hitting the 8-ball, like 'you have to bank the cue ball five times', or 'you need to do a jump shot.' I could randomly bank the cue ball multiple times without ever hitting the 8- ball, but these guys had strategy. Hoot's dad was the reigning champ in the park, and he retained his title after playing that night.

I stayed for a long weekend and then flew back to Iowa to find 9" of fresh snow on the ground. Hoot stayed another week and drove back alone.

Chapter 11
More Changes

‘‘Do you know anyone who wants to buy an apartment building?” Hoot asked one day in April 2005. It had been over a year since our trip to see his parents and almost three years since the initial PSA test. He had been trying to address his health concerns on his own by eating healthier and exercising more, but he seemed to be moving more carefully.

"Which one are you selling?"

"I have a 6 plex and a 4 plex. I want to sell the 6 plex. It's taking too much of my time. I want to slow down and enjoy life more."

"I understand that, but any chance the pain in your back is making it tough to keep up?" I asked.

"No. The pain in my back is just knotted muscles. I need to exercise more. I like to work hard and play hard. I still work hard, I just want more time to play.

'Whatever you say," I said. I didn't agree with his decisions about his health but there was nothing I could do about it other than express my concern. He was 52 years old and would make his own decisions no matter what I thought.

"Do you have anyone interested in buying?" I asked.

"Actually I have a few nibbles. I think I'll sell my house too and move into an open apartment in my 4 plex. The 4 plex has a heated double garage that I could turn into my shop. It will be good to have room to spread out my woodworking tools. Time to make some changes."

It was time to make some changes in my life, too. Hoot and I still talked often and visited occasionally but our relationship had clearly changed. A mutual friend told me that Hoot had stopped seeing the woman he met while speed dating and was now seeing someone else. I wasn't interested in dating so soon and wanted space in my personal life, but I was interested in making a change in my professional life so I looked around for school counseling jobs and ended up accepting a position 200 miles away in a large school district near Des Moines, Iowa. I put my house up for sale and planned to move in a few months.

Hoot accomplished his housing changes quickly but his physical movement was slowing down. It was clear he wasn't feeling well but he continued to refuse additional medical treatment and spent time in his new boat floating on a quiet river watching turkey vultures ride the thermals or working on projects in his shop. He was adding power tools to his collection since he had room to expand, so a lathe was added to the table saw, chop saw, and planer among other related tools, and he was looking forward to working with some exotic woods that were being delivered. Then early in June 2005 I received a phone call.

"Got a minute?" Hoot asked.

"Always," I said, grateful for a break from packing.

"I wasn't going to call, but I figured you'd be mad if I didn't tell you."

"Tell me what?"

"I'm in the hospital."

"Cuz why?"

"Would you believe I'm a victim of a hit and run?"

"No."

"Shot myself in the foot?"

"Maybe."

"How about I fell down the stairs?"

"More likely," I said. "I notice you've been having trouble walking, and I've seen your walking stick near the door. So why are you in the hospital?"

"You're right about trouble walking, and isn't that a cool stick? It's made out of wood called diamond willow. I noticed a problem with my legs awhile ago. I've been doing everything I could think of to strengthen them but they're getting weaker. Early this morning I tried to get out of bed but my legs wouldn't support me. I finally hobbled and crawled to my truck and drove to the emergency room."

"Why didn't you call me?" I asked.

"I knew you'd say that. What could you have done?"

"Probably called an ambulance."

"Exactly. And do you know how much they cost? It was way cheaper to drive myself. I was OK sitting, I just couldn't walk. It was just the opposite of your back problem when you could walk but couldn't sit. Besides, there's less traffic early in the morning so it's safer."

"Do you want some company?" I asked.

"I'd like that," he said. "And would you mind

bringing along a jar of crunchy peanut butter? I'm guessing they only have creamy and that will be a problem tomorrow morning."

"You're obsessed with crunchy peanut butter, but yes, I'll bring some along."

Arriving at the hospital it was clear that the pain meds he had been given were taking effect. "Hey," Hoot said, behind deeply lidded eyes.

"I'm here," I said, putting the peanut butter on the bedside tray.

"I can see that."

"So what's the plan?"

"They're doing a bunch of tests. No results yet. Hurry up and wait. I'm supposed to know more by tomorrow afternoon."

"Are you hurting?"

"Not any more," he replied. "These meds are good shit! If I could take these at home I wouldn't need to pay for a hospital bed, and I could eat breakfast at home."

"Let's see what tomorrow brings," I said, kissing his forehead as he fell asleep. "Sweet dreams!

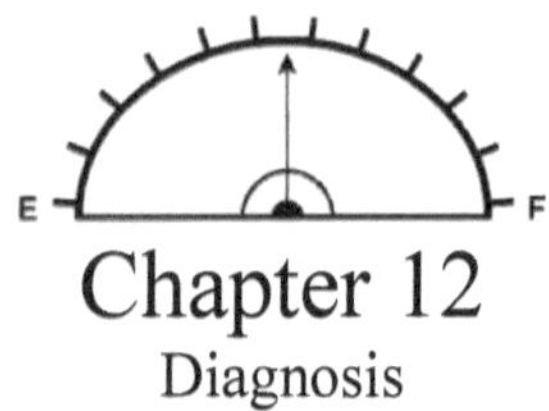

Chapter 12
Diagnosis

"Evidently I have prostate cancer," Hoot told me when I saw him the next afternoon.

"What finally convinced you?"

"The pictures convinced me. I have a large tumor wrapped around the middle of my spine called the thoracic area. That's what's been causing my back ache and making trouble for my legs."

I felt a lump in my gut. "So now what?"

"They want to do surgery to get rid of the tumor."

"Are you OK with that?" I almost expected him to sign out of the hospital against medical advice and go home.

"I guess so, my PSA is close to 200. I still think their test is wrong, but I can't argue with the pictures. Surgery is tomorrow. My parents and brothers will be here soon.

As I was getting ready for bed that night I heard a song by Tim McGraw titled 'Live Like You Were Dying'. I'd heard it before, but it really hit home this time, and I cried myself to sleep.

"I was in my early 40's with a lot of life before me,
When a moment came that stopped me on a dime.
I spent most of the next days looking at the x-rays
Talkin' 'bout the options, and talkin' 'bout sweet time".

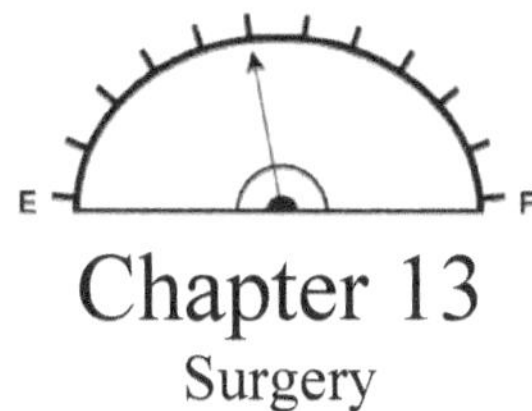

Chapter 13
Surgery

“Are you here for Steve?” the surgeon asked. All of us in the waiting room nodded like bobble head dolls. “Steve has prostate cancer which has metastasized into bone cancer. He had a massive and aggressive malignant tumor wrapped around his spine. We removed as much as we could and he will need chemo and radiation to get rid of the rest. The tumor has done a lot of damage and eaten away at the vertebra so we fused T5-9 and added two titanium rods to give him support. This will greatly reduce his flexibility, but he will still be able to walk. Other than the obvious, Steve is in good health and at age 52 he is still young. That is to his advantage, but there is no cure for bone cancer. I would predict he has about two good years left. It's especially sad because it didn't need to be this way.” Looking pointedly at the men in the room he said, “Gentlemen, get your PSA checked. It's a simple blood test. Get medical help if there's a problem.”

Then looking at all of us he added, “Do you have any questions?”

We sat in shocked silence as the surgeon left. Tears and hugs passed the time until we could see Steve. The men made appointments for PSA tests. Massive and aggressive tumor? Bone cancer? Two years? Our lives changed that afternoon. So did Steve's.

Steve was eventually released from the hospital and I stopped by his home to help however I could. He spent most of the day sitting in a recliner while wearing a brace from his waist to his armpits. It was molded to his front and back, attached with heavy duty Velcro, and reminded me of a turtle shell. The purpose was to support his back while it healed.

"Hi Steve, how are you doing?"

"Oh, pretty good, I guess. This brace is hot, but I need it for a while. Thanks for helping me out in the afternoons."

"You're welcome. I'm glad I can help until your friend comes after work." I had heard from a mutual acquaintance that his new girlfriend came by after work to help him in the evenings.

"So you're really going to move?" he asked.

"Yes, I am. I know the timing stinks, but I'll be back to visit if that's OK."

"You bet," he said. In the weeks that followed I spent a great deal of time with him. We would talk about our trips, or he would walk me through completing minor repair jobs, or I made meals for the freezer that he could use as needed, like he had done for me a few years earlier. With each passing day the calendar got closer to my moving date.

The day of my move finally happened in late July 2005. It was now a four hour trip to visit in person so Steve and I stayed in touch through phone calls and emails.

A few weeks later the students were almost ready to return to school when he called with a request.

"Promise to just think about what I'm going to say. Don't give me an answer, OK?"

"OK," I said, with no clue of where this was going.

"I know you just started your new job, and I'm still recovering from this surgery, but I have an idea. You and I have always traveled well together, haven't we?"

"Yes."

"I have an idea and please don't say no right away, promise to think about it, ok?"

"OK."

"The surgeon said I have about two good years left so I was thinking I would sell everything I have and buy an RV. You quit teaching and we'll travel for as long as I can handle it. You'll probably need to help me toward the end. When I'm gone, everything I have will be yours. Then you could return to teaching again if you wanted."

I was quiet for a while, letting his suggestion sink in, as well as noting that he was actually listening to his doctor.

"You promised to think about it, remember?" Steve said.

"I'll think about it, but one snag in your plan is that if I quit my job now I could lose my teaching license."

"How do you figure that?"

"I signed a contract for a year, I just started this new job, and the students come in a few days. Leaving teaching isn't as simple as giving a two week notice. I'm expected to be here for the year. If I leave early I would be fined, probably about $1,000, and if they wanted to play hard ball they could pull my license which means I couldn't teach again."

"You've talked before about maybe getting out of teaching."

"Yes, but that would be by my choice, not because I didn't have a license anymore."

"I don't think they'd really pull your license. That sounds like a pretty extreme situation. But back to my idea. Will you promise to think about it?"

"Sure. Let's talk about it in a few days."

Later in the week we talked again.

"Steve, I've been thinking about your idea with the RV."

"You're going to say no, aren't you?"

"Correct, and here's why. If circumstances were different then I think it could work, but between my new job and your health problems I don't think this is a good idea."

"My time is limited, Mary, and even though I think I'll outlive their two year prediction I'm not sure how this is all going to end. Evidently bone cancer is terminal."

"Life is terminal, Hoot, but I know what you mean. Neither of us have any idea the type of care you will need and as much as we both like to travel, now is not the time to be looking for cancer treatment in the yellow pages if you have medical trouble on the road. Remember how worried you were when I took the dune buggy up too high off a sand dune? Now we're talking about something much more serious."

"Yeah, I thought about health care too, but it's more fun to think about the traveling part."

"Maybe we can do a weekend camping trip sometime if you feel up to it."

"I'm not sure I can sleep on the ground anymore, but camping for a weekend is probably safer than traveling for the next two years. You have to admit this was a good idea."

"It was a great idea, Hoot!"

"I decided I'm going to buy another bike," he added.

"Really? What kind?"

"Actually I'm going to buy two more. One is a Suzuki Bergman step through. It's a motorcycle but I don't have to swing my leg over it to get on which is why it's called a step through. It should be easier for me when I'm done with all these treatments. I plan to ride the Wing and the Harley again, but it might take awhile before I can get my leg over the seat. The other is a recumbent bicycle. I can use that to strengthen my legs."

"Good for you, Hoot. I'm glad you're looking ahead." I said.

His treatments continued as needed while he went through chemo and radiation. Fortunately he had a strong support system of friends nearby. During one particular conversation he sounded exhausted, and I tried to change the topic to something I hoped he was still able to enjoy. "You're still using your Big Green Egg to grill, right?

"No, I'm not doing much grilling right now," Steve said.

"You love grilling on the Egg, why have you stopped?"

"When you get radiation it burns the flesh. Burnt skin looks like raw meat and smells like raw meat, so grilling raw meat just doesn't sound good right now.

Next year will be better. This sucks. My bowels are all messed up because that area is where they aim the radiation. This isn't living, this is just existing. Maybe it will get better but right now it's hard to see the future so I've been thinking. I wondered if it really gets bad, would you help me check out early?"

It took me a moment to comprehend what he was asking. "I love you, Hoot. And if it gets really bad I won't stand in your way, but I won't help you."

"I figured that's what you'd say. Let's hope it doesn't come to that."

Chapter 14
Legend

By the time a few months had passed Hoot celebrated his 53rd birthday and his life had changed dramatically. Instead of refusing to see doctors he had become a regular at the cancer center. Instead of wading through flooded basements to fix a water heater he was walking at the pool to strengthen his legs at the same gym where we used to play racquetball.

"I go to the pool three times a week," he told me one day.

"Does it take too much out of you to go every day?"

"No, I could go every day, but I only go on the days they have water aerobics."

"You're doing water aerobics now?"

"Hell no, I'm just trying to walk without holding onto the edge of the pool, but you should see the instructor! She's a cutie, and it's a bonus that she's wearing a swimsuit! I just wish she'd get in the water before she starts teaching on the side of the pool. Even with a dry suit, she's still way better looking than all the old women with their flabby arms."

Steve's treatments were attacking the cancer, but his PSA continued to climb. "Did you know I'm a legend?" Steve mentioned one day.

"Do I want to know why?"

"When I walked into the cancer center, one of the nurses said 'here comes the legend!' I asked what she was talking about. Evidently one of the doctors had been talking about my PSA numbers and said he'd never seen a man with a PSA in the 500's who was still walking around. I never thought I'd be a legend, but here I am, killing it!!"

I'm not sure he recognized the irony of that statement.

Chapter 15
Orchi

His back surgery had been in June 2005, and at that time the surgeon predicted Hoot had two good years left. He had completed chemo and radiation and it was now 2007. His two years were up, but there was an escape route to buy more time.

"I'm having more surgery," Steve mentioned one evening.

"On your back?"

"No. This one is called an orchiectomy."

"Excuse me?"

"It's called an 'orchi' for short."

"I know ectomy means to remove but what is the orchi they are removing?"

"Orchiectomy is the removal of the testicles," he explained.

What's the right response to that statement?

"I don't know what to say."

"That's a first! I tell you I'm being castrated and you have nothing to say?"

"Why are they removing your testicles?" I finally asked.

"Remember that the surgeon said I had about two good years left? I'm at the end of that line but I can buy more time. The testicles produce testosterone which feeds prostate cancer like adding gas to a fire.

That's why my PSA number keeps climbing. Removal of the testicles doesn't remove the cancer, but it does slow its growth. I've always known castration was an option but I've never been willing to consider it. Funny what choices we make when our back is against the wall. I asked the doctor if they would remove the prostate, but he said no because it's like closing the barn door after the horse has left. This gives a whole new meaning to rocky mountain oysters. Maybe surgery could be called a Hooter Neuter!"

"You seem to be taking it pretty well," I said.

"Yeah, at least the doctor agreed to put them in a jar for me to take home."

"Excuse me?"

"I won't be able to have sex anymore, but I could still reach in the jar to scratch my balls every morning!"

I was afraid he was serious.

"So how did it go?" I asked after he was released from the surgery.

"It took longer to numb me up than the actual surgery. I had to put my feet in stirrups. I know you women have to do that, but it is definitely not a natural position for a guy. The stirrups were the most uncomfortable part until I heard my balls hit the bucket they had sitting on a table. It was a very simple surgery for something so dramatic. This sure as hell better work."

A few weeks later I asked if he could tell any difference.

"Absolutely! My PSA has dropped to zero. I had no idea hormones were such a big part of our personality. I can tell something is different because when I see a pretty girl on the street I don't look twice anymore, and the water aerobics coach doesn't keep my attention like she used to."

"Any idea how much time this surgery may have given you?"

"The surgeon said it gave me as much as two extra years and I have a goal to prove them wrong and outlive their estimates. I intend to live for whatever time I have left, not just sit and wait to die. Have you ever heard the Tim McGraw song, 'Live Like You Were Dying?'"

Oh yeah, I knew all about that song and its message. Hoot and I always got along well, but I never knew what to expect of his physical condition when I called or went to visit. Some days he was great. Other days, not so much.

"I wish I had dental insurance," he told me one day. "A side effect of all the chemo and radiation is problems with my teeth. I'd like to pull them all and get dentures but do you have any idea what that costs?"

"I've noticed your teeth have gotten dark. Does it bother you to eat?"

"Kind of. It depends on what I'm eating of course. Crunchy peanut butter is still OK, thank God. You know how I hate creamy peanut butter."

"I know. You're a fanatic."

"Yes, but I'm a loveable fanatic."

I couldn't argue that point.

Chapter 16
Hospice

Steve reached his 55th birthday in 2007. I visited him every few months and it seemed like he was feeling as well as possible. He said he was more tired than usual but was having a good time working in his shop or spending time with friends. That started to change after he turned 56 in the fall of 2008.

"My doctor is a prick," Hoot said in what would become increasingly frequent phone calls. "He was on vacation for a while, so I'd been seeing someone else for my last few appointments. When my doctor walked in today he looked surprised and said 'You're still here? I thought you'd be dead by now.' What the hell!"

It occurred to me that Steve's initial back surgery had happened in 2005. They gave him two years which were up in 2007. Then he had his orchiectomy in 2007 which supposedly gave him another two years. Those two years would end in 2009. Right now it was the fall of 2008. I could understand why the doctor would be surprised, but agreed that the comment was rude and totally unprofessional.

"What did you say?" I asked.

"Once upon a time I would have balled up my fists

and walked out, but that was then and this is now. I asked him if he was disappointed I was still alive. He said as sick as I am he was surprised I was still walking but damn, he didn't need to be so rude about it. Then he asked if I'd thought about hospice. Evidently he thinks I'm going to die soon. I looked into it just to see what it's about. Did you know that once I'm approved for hospice, then all the medical bills associated with my cancer are paid?"

"Nope. I don't know much about hospice." I suspected there was some arrangement for him to be approved for Medicare as well as hospice, I was just glad it wasn't coming out of his pocket.

"I didn't either, but I do now. Hospice offers a variety of services and the one I could really use is routine home care. It will help a lot! This doctor was the only one who ever said point blank the end is near. It's been four years since my back surgery. There are some days that are worse than others, but I'm not dead yet! He's still a prick, and I'm not dying anytime soon, but he referred me to hospice so they check on me at home, and payment for my meds are covered. Going to the cancer center all the time takes a lot of energy that I don't always have. It will be nice for a nurse to come to me."

Chapter 17
Legalities

"I've had something on my mind I wanted to ask you," I said during a call in the spring of 2009.

"Log cabin plans? Air conditioner parts? Hooter Scooter trips?" he suggested.

"I have files of log cabin plans, and my knowledge of air conditioners doesn't go too far past the thermostat, but I've wondered if you're getting your affairs in order."

"Not you, too." He sounded frustrated. "I'm not ready to check out yet. There's plenty of time to get serious about all that legal stuff."

"Have you at least thought about it?"

"Yeah, but not much. When I'm having a good day I want to be out on my boat watching turkey vultures ride the thermals, or in my shop working on all the projects I've got in mind. I even went out for another flight last week. It was good to be in the air for an hour. When I'm having a bad day then I'm sleeping. I don't want to spend time thinking about dying."

"An hour is all it would take to get the process started," I suggested. "You have a friend who is a notary. At least it would make sure your wishes are documented. You've worked so hard for everything you have, don't you want to give things to people who will appreciate what you've worked for? Have you thought about selling your motorcycles? I know you need to keep your truck, and you still use your boat and some tools, but what about selling the apartment building?"

"Will you get off my back if I tell you I have a will?"

"Really? When did you do that?" I assumed he had done it recently, but I was wrong.

"About 30 years ago," he said.

"Seriously? Over three decades?" It was my turn to be frustrated.

"I left everything I have to an old girlfriend. We broke up, obviously, and she married some guy. I never changed the will because I just never got around to it, and there's an expense involved. Besides, she knew about it and sent me a letter verifying that she doesn't want anything that I have. Her letter should be enough."

"'Should' doesn't sound very definite. Where's the letter?"

"The letter is in my file cabinet and the will is in my safety deposit box. I've already made arrangements for my bikes and a few other things to go to some of my buddies, and I promise to write up some ideas of who should get what. I'm guessing you'd like the Big Green Egg?"

I wanted to ask more questions but he obviously didn't want to talk about it, and ultimately it wasn't any of my business.

"The Egg is a poor substitute for you, but sure, it will bring back good memories."

"You might need some lessons on how to grill

without burning everything."

"I'll practice. Can I come to visit next weekend and maybe you can show me?"

"Sure, I'm not going anywhere and now I'm going to bed. See you soon."

Chapter 18
Moosefart

The next Friday night, April 11, 2009, I walked into his home and we exchanged a hug. In true Hoot fashion he took the opportunity to tickle my ribs and, as always, I flinched.

"I still got it!" He grinned.

"Yeah, I guess some things never change," I said while walking into the kitchen for a glass of water. Contrary to my comment a number of things had changed, starting with the daily med container. It had grown since I'd last seen it and instead of just one row with the days of the week, it had morphed into jumbo size for morning, noon and evening of each day of the week. Each slot was full of pills. A booklet about hospice was on the counter with the name and phone number of his hospice nurse on the cover. Then I saw the jar of creamy peanut butter. I walked back to him holding the jar in the air. "What's this? Since when did you start eating creamy peanut butter?"

His eyes were wet as he looked at me. "Since crunchy peanut butter started hurting my teeth."

My eyes started leaking. That simple statement about peanut butter made it all too real. Cancer was slowly claiming his body piece by piece. And was it my imagination, or was his left eye starting to bulge out? That might explain the eye drops I saw in the kitchen. I put the peanut butter back on the counter without another comment.

We spent Saturday running a few errands which included shopping at K-Mart for tennis shoes that fastened with Velcro since he couldn't bend to tie his shoes. He was waving his walking stick to catch the motion activated entrance doors when we both saw the motorized shopping carts. "Wanna ride?" he asked, raising his eyebrows.

I stood on the back as he drove us around the aisles of K-Mart. We were laughing and crying and then laughing more as he navigated turns like they were backroads and went around merchandise on the floor like it was roadkill. It was a variation on the Hooter Scooter. If we'd been teenagers I'm sure we would have been reprimanded, but people just looked at us, shook their heads, rolled their eyes and left us alone. We found the shoes, picked up some groceries and then went back to his home. I wanted to soak up every moment. The errands had tired him out. He sat in his recliner and closed his eyes.

"Would you rub lotion into my feet?" he asked. "My skin gets so dry from the meds and with that rod in my back I can't bend to reach past my knees anymore."

"Sure," I sat on the floor and started applying lotion. His feet were dry and flaky. "This reminds me of rubbing suntan lotion on your back during some of our trips."

"We had some great times, didn't we? I really appreciate you making a copy of the scrapbook because it brings back so many memories. Which trip was your favorite?"

"I enjoyed them all but my favorite was in 2000 when we headed west with no real plan in mind. I can't believe we were on the road for 24 days! I loved Yellowstone and Hoback Junction and white-water rafting. How about you, Hoot? Which trip was your favorite?"

"I liked that one, too. All of my buddies are jealous because they want to hit the open road and just ride until they decide to turn around and go home. I'm living proof that you can't postpone everything until retirement. I still have to laugh about the trip we took up to Flin Flon, Canada. Do you remember that it is so far north the road literally ends at Flin Flon? If you want to go farther north, you have to take a plane."

"I will remember the lesson I learned on that trip for a long time, specifically that the sun sets a lot later the farther north you drive!"

Steve was relaxed as I continued rubbing lotion and soon he started snoring. I finished with the lotion and moved a chair next to the recliner so I was facing him when he woke up.

"Sorry I fell asleep, I was dreaming about our kayak trip on the Upper Iowa River, remember?"

"Yes. And I remember falling asleep on the back of the bike when we traveled on a warm day. You always said you could tell when I fell asleep because I leaned forward and my helmet hit yours. And I remember dancing in the back seat when you cranked up the tunes on a deserted highway. We've had a lot of good times, Hoot." I was sitting beside him with my hand on his arm. When had it become so frail and the skin so loose? I wanted to hold his hand but was afraid I'd hurt him.

"We've had a lot of great times," he corrected, "and I'm glad we had them when we did, because I think my great times are over." There was a finality in his voice. "I don't know how much time I have left. I keep thinking I can beat this thing but it's been almost four years since I was diagnosed and it's finally catching up with me. My last hope is for a miracle but I've never gone to church so I don't think that will happen. I did get baptized recently after one of my friends talked me into it. I had to kneel in a stock tank. The water was cold and the bottom of the tank was slimy. The minister kept talking and pouring water over me. I was wrinkled when I finally got out, but it seemed like a good thing to do."

"I'm glad you are baptized, Steve, but I don't think church attendance has anything to do with miracles," I said. "I'll keep praying for you."

"Thanks," he said. "I suppose praying can't hurt, and it might help."

After a few moments of quiet Hoot seemed to gather strength to continue the conversation. "Remember when I came to your house to fix your air conditioner? You weren't any good at racquetball but you sure got my attention when you started talking about a log cabin."

"You got my attention when you suggested I take you out to dinner."

"Yeah, I've gotten a lot of mileage out of that repair job."

We looked at each other as the mood subtly shifted from playful to serious. We both seemed to recognize that there wouldn't be many more opportunities to talk.

"We've had a lot of great times together," he said again, reaching for my hand, "and we've had our differences, but I've never stopped loving you. You know that, right?"

"I know, Steve. My love for you has changed over the years, but I still love you, too."

He nodded. "I've fought as hard as I can, but cancer is winning. I don't have many regrets. I've lived a full life and followed my dreams. It's time for you to follow yours."

My eyes got wet and my cheeks turned hot as I heard him admit that his life was coming to an end. I wanted to squeeze his hand but stopped, pretty sure that it would cause pain.

He rested for a moment before adding, "You know that your dreams are off the beaten path, right? You want a log cabin with a great view, not a fancy home with a white picket fence in the suburbs. I always wanted to build you that cabin but you can still make it happen. I'm going to leave you enough money to help finance the bulk of the cost. Build it in Montana, or the Carolina's, or Colorado, hell, build it in Moosefart, USA just build the damn thing! If you settle for less then I'll come back and haunt you! Life is like money, you can spend it anyway you want, but you can only spend it once. I think Benjamin Franklin said that. It's still true. Figure out a way to travel and write as much as you want. And I'd like you to write my story so some other schmuck doesn't make the same stupid mistakes I made by waiting so damn long to get help."

"I'll write your story," I said as tears ran down my

cheeks. "But you don't have to haunt me, you can just come and visit."

"What do you think is on the other side?" he asked.

"I don't know for sure, Hoot, but I believe there is something there and that it is good."

"Yeah, I think so too."

"I do believe in people coming back in some form or another," I continued. "Not physically, but in spirit. I know sometimes I feel the presence of my dad or my aunt and it makes me feel good, like they're with me."

"If you die before me then you can come and visit, and if I die first then I'll come and visit. Deal?"

"Deal," I agreed.

"And another thing," he said.

"What's that?"

"The quilt you made me has kept me warm many nights. Make sure you take it home with you when I don't need it anymore."

"Deal," I said again.

We shared a smile and a long gaze. We held hands as he closed his eyes and fell asleep again.

The next morning was Sunday and he was bright eyed and full of life. "What a beautiful day!" he said. "I feel great!"

It was obvious that he was moving easier and more comfortably than the day before. "Your body must feel like it's on a roller coaster," I said.

"Yeah, some days, like yesterday, are tough, but today I feel invincible!"

"You know I need to leave in a few hours," I reminded him.

"Yeah, I know. Do you want to go out for a bite to

eat?" he asked. "I'll let you buy in honor of not only having reached my 56th birthday, but I'm halfway to 57! A lot of people didn't think I'd make it this far."

"What a perfect reason to celebrate. Let's go!" I grabbed the creamy peanut butter on the way out the door.

Two hours later we were back from his favorite breakfast spot and I was packing up to head home. Steve was still in good spirits, but tiring. His mind had places to go and things to do but his body wasn't cooperating so a nap was on his afternoon agenda.

"Stay in touch! Think about Moosefart!" He tickled my ribs as we hugged and I flinched. How could he always zero in on the exact spot that caused a reaction? He smiled with satisfaction.

"I'll be back in a few weeks, Hoot," I was grateful that he was having a good day, but wondered how long it would last.

"OK, I'll rest up so we can go out to eat again."

"See you soon," I walked to my car, hoping that I would get the chance to see him again. About four hours later my phone rang as I arrived home.

"I just woke up from my nap and am making sure you got home OK," Hoot said.

"Perfect timing. I just walked in the house."

"Hey, I meant to ask you, what ever happened to that girl, Caprice?"

"She found me last year through the web site of the church where I play piano. She sent an email to the pastor and asked him to forward it to me. She was almost done with college and was planning her wedding. We met and it was great to catch up with her."

"Wow! How cool is that!"

"Agreed! How was your nap?"

"Great! And I'm still feeling good. I need to take advantage of this so I'm calling a few of my buddies to catch up with them. Thanks again for coming over this weekend. It was great to see you."

"Great to see you, too, Steve," I said. "Talk to you soon?"

"You bet. Bye!"

His voice still had energy in it the next few times I talked to him and I was glad he seemed to have some relief. That changed when I called the following Sunday.

Chapter 19
Hospital

Someone answered the phone but it wasn't Hoot. I recognized the voice of one of his friends.

"Mary, thanks for calling. I have Hoot's phone, he was trying to talk but wasn't making sense so I called 911 and the ambulance just left. How soon can you get here?"

"On my way," I made arrangements to cover a few commitments, and when I pulled into the hospital parking lot a few hours later I tried to compose myself for what I expected to be a difficult visit. I walked inside, found the right floor and was leaving the elevator when I recognized some of the former racquetball players walking toward me. We briefly shook hands and exchanged quick hugs. Their cheeks were wet, no words were necessary. I walked down the hallway, slowing as the room numbers got closer to Steve's. Taking a deep breath I turned into his room.

Hoot saw me and smiled. He looked so small in the bed. His left eye was definitely bulging out along with some red tissue in the corner of the eye socket. His arms were even skinnier than last week, and he was receiving oxygen through a nasal cannula. His family and close friends were already there. I choked back tears and reached for his hand but he pulled me in for a hug then tickled my ribs. There was no strength in his fingers so I faked a flinch.

I saw his satisfied grin.

"You still got it," I said for him.

He smiled and laid back on the pillow. We looked at each other for a while as the others in the room seemed to fade away. Hoot was struggling to speak so I said, "I think we said everything we needed to say last week, didn't we? He nodded, but then his facial expressions grew concerned and he tried to sit up. I realized we would need to play a variation on the game of twenty questions.

"Is something bothering you?"

A nod. Yes.

"Are you hurting?"

No.

"Are you wondering what happened?"

Yes.

"Today is Sunday. You were in your home earlier this morning and one of your friends had stopped by. Evidently you were talking but not making any sense. They called an ambulance that brought you to the hospital. You've been here most of the day. You are receiving oxygen to help you breathe easier. A lot of people have been called so there's probably been old friends stopping by that you haven't seen in a while. Your parents and brothers are already here."

He nodded, and I continued with a few more questions.

"Are you worried about what's happening?"

No.

"Are you worried that this all happened quicker than

you thought and your affairs aren't in order?"

Definite yes.

I tried to push the current situation aside in order to remember our conversations about this. "You said you would create a list about dividing your things, did you do that?"

Yes.

"Is it in your file cabinet?"

No.

"Is it on your computer?"

Yes.

"Is it labeled so I can find it easily?"

Yes.

"Do you want me to go to your home and print it off?

Definite yes.

"Is there more?"

Yes.

I could tell there was something else on his mind but I couldn't think of what to ask. Hoot finally laid back on the bed, his energy was spent. I couldn't get over how small he looked on the hospital bed.

"OK, I'll stick around here for a while and then one of your buddies and I will go to your home and do what we can to help."

He nodded and smiled.

I looked at him through my tears and tried to commit his face to memory. "Come back and visit me if that's allowed. I love you, Steve," I kissed his forehead.

He nodded again, gave me an air kiss, and fell asleep.

A nurse came in to take his vitals but the blood pressure cuff seemed to cause pain so we requested that she stop because what was the point?

Chapter 20
Final Wishes

I spoke to Hoot's best friend, Shane, about what I needed to do. He was glad to hear of my plans because he needed to carry out another request from Hoot.

"If I ever can't get back home," Hoot had told him more than once, "get the pot out of the house!"

Arriving at Hoot's home I knew exactly where I needed to go. Shane wasn't sure where to start but he had a few ideas.

I found the document titled "Final Wishes" on Hoot's desktop and printed it off. He had specified who was to get his belongings, but I doubted that most of his wishes could be honored. He had listed a few sentimental items like he wanted the quilt and the Egg to go home with me, but most of his wishes appeared legal in nature. Since it wasn't notarized there was no way to prove these were Steve's wishes and not something that I or anyone else just typed up. Shane found stashes of pot in the bottom drawer of the file cabinet, above a ceiling tile, and in a floor safe. We left the house with a single sheet of paper and a large Ziplock bag packed with a green leafy substance that we set inside in a paper grocery bag. "I have never followed every single traffic law like I did in the time it took me to get that bag home!" Shane told me later.

I showed the document of his final wishes to Steve's brothers. They also questioned the legality of his intentions, so the next day we made arrangements to have a lawyer review it and see if there was any way to get the document notarized. The lawyer asked a few questions about Hoot's medical condition, and his opinion was brief and to the point. Based on the fact that Hoot had been receiving heavy pain medication was enough to invalidate anything Steve would sign or say. Additionally, Hoot's current incoherent state of mind further invalidated any legal action.

Some of what Hoot was requesting on the document couldn't be honored because it was a change of beneficiary which could only be done through a signed contract with the specific company. This included his wish that I be named the beneficiary on his life insurance policy. Hoot had named an executor but the letter wasn't notarized so it held no legal weight. He had also named specific people who were to get the apartment building and other items, but that involved signing titles and other legalities. The lawyer explained that the only thing this document was worth was to provide Steve's family with his wishes, assuming Steve's possessions were transferred to his family. It all hinged on the will.

Then, like a nagging thought that finally worked itself into consciousness, it occurred to me the last thing Hoot had on his mind: find the letter from the old girlfriend about the will. I mentioned it to the lawyer.

The lawyer explained that if the original will naming the girlfriend was in the safety deposit box, and no other will was produced, then the original will would be followed. If the letter from the girlfriend was produced and it specified that she wanted nothing, then Hoot's family would likely be awarded the contents of his estate, starting with his parents and then his brothers. If a more recent will was produced then it would be followed. We went back to the house but we couldn't find the letter. No one else had access to his safety deposit box so we didn't know if there were any surprises there. The box would be opened after Steve's death. In the meantime the sentimental items were gathered to be distributed according to Hoot's wishes. We had done all we could. All that was left to do was wait.

Chapter 21
Solo Trip - 2009

Returning to the hospital, Steve's condition was changing quickly. His ability to respond and see were now compromised. "There is a tumor behind his eye that has been pushing his eyeball and eye tissue out. It's moving into the brain and will affect his vital organs," we were told. "It won't be long."

Hoot slipped into a coma surrounded by people who loved him. He died the next day, Tuesday, April 21, 2009. It was just a few weeks shy of 4 years since his initial diagnosis. He was 56 years old.

Chapter 22
Hilltop

"Is anybody here religious?" The question was asked to no one in particular. About fifteen of Hoot's family and friends were standing around his grave in a cemetery on a hilltop, overlooking a valley lush with trees leafing out for the year. Songbirds provided music for the occasion.

Some of the guys kicked the ground under their feet. Others cleared their throats. Eyes were wet. Hoot had been cremated and although he wanted to donate his organs the only part of him viable for donation was the right eye which was given to the Lions Club. The rest of Hoot was in a small box built by his brother with exotic wood that Hoot had given him.

"It was starting to sink in that Steve was gone, because usually when I built something Steve would come around and tell me what I was doing wrong. This time he kept quiet!" his brother said.

A scripture verse was recited, and I shared one of Hoot's favorite phrases penned by Hunter S. Thompson, "Life should not be a journey to the grave with the intention of arriving safely in a pretty and well preserved body, but rather to skid in broadside in a cloud of smoke, thoroughly used up, totally worn out, and loudly proclaiming 'Wow! What a Ride!'"

Rest in peace, Hoot.

Chapter 23
Finale and Call to Action

The safety deposit box was drilled open in the presence of one of Hoot's brothers. The box held the will dated from 30 years ago but nothing more recent, and the brother was escorted out. The letter written by the old girlfriend was never found, and though she may have told Hoot she didn't want his things, it was now many years later and she was married. She might not have wanted Hoot's things, but evidently her husband did and he got a windfall; specifically the four-plex apartment building and other items probably totaling hundreds of thousands of dollars in total assets. Hoot had told me that he'd always bought the best he could afford of the things he wanted, and now those things were handed to a girl he hadn't seen in over 30 years and a total stranger.

Hoot's dad was the beneficiary to the life insurance policy. His parents were getting older and were able to put the monies to good use, which is the way it should be.

Hoot's reason for never updating his will? "I'll do it later."

Advice Hoot would probably offer:
(This is food for thought and not meant to take the place of official legal or medical advice.)

• If you don't have health insurance, at least consider catastrophic insurance. Medical care is expensive.

• If something in your body doesn't feel right, don't procrastinate too long before getting it checked out. Suck it up and make an appointment.

• Make an appointment with a lawyer. You might think lawyers are only necessary when you're old or sick, but accidents happen. Pandemics happen. Make sure your spouse, children, possessions are cared for. Pre-pay for burial if possible.

• Don't assume everything will be left to your spouse...what if you die together? Check your beneficiaries in policies occasionally to make sure nothing has changed.

• If making or changing a will is not something you want to do, at least write up your wishes and **get that piece of paper notarized**. There may be a small fee. This can be done at your local bank or public library as well as many other places. Keep that paper in a safe place. Take a few hours out of your life and get 'er done. When you're laying in a hospital bed with only a few hours left to live you don't want to regret not taking care of things when you had the chance.

• If you have a safety deposit box then consider having another signer on the box. For a small fee you can have more than two signers. It may seem like overkill, but it might be worth the peace of mind.

- **Upon death:** Upon death nothing will matter to you anymore, but your will and any notarized documents become very important to those left behind.
- **Not dead yet?** If you're breathing then you are legally responsible for your bills. You also make your own decisions about medical care, and due to confidentiality rules no one else is to know anything about your health details. So make arrangements for two things: someone to help with finances and someone to help with health. Why? Because if you're incapacitated due to being critically injured or seriously ill, but you're still breathing, then someone else can help out.
  - Financial power of attorney: This person would have the legal authority to make financial decisions on your behalf: like making sure your monthly bills get paid, or talking to your insurance company if your roof has storm damage, and other types of assistance until you recover to resume these duties yourself. In a worst case scenario and you never recover then this person would have authorization to sell your home, vehicle, etc. Once you stop breathing then the directives in your will take over.
  - Medical power of attorney: This person would have the legal authority to make medical decisions on your behalf; like discussing treatments, approving surgery, and talking to medical personnel. In a worst case scenario this

person would have authorization to stop all treatment and ask medical personnel to keep you comfortable until death. This is different than a living will. Learn the difference.

○ Choose these people carefully. Then make sure they have the information they would need to carry out their role if it would ever be necessary.

What are you waiting for? *Get moving!* I wanted Mary to write this so other guys don't make stupid choices like I did. If my story didn't teach you anything else, I hope you understand that time is like money. You can spend it however you want, but you can only spend it once. Make it count.

Symptoms of Prostate Cancer
(from Center for Disease Control/CDC)

- Difficulty starting urination.
- Weak or interrupted flow of urine.
- Frequent urination, especially at night.
- Difficulty emptying the bladder completely.
- Pain or burning during urination.
- Blood in the urine or semen.
- Erectile dysfunction.
- Pain in the back, hips, or pelvis that doesn't go away.
- Painful ejaculation.
- Decreased force in the stream of urine.
- Bone pain.

About the Author

Mary Snyder is still working as a school counselor but getting closer to retirement every day! She grew up in Storm Lake, Iowa, and is currently living in Ankeny, Iowa, with her dog, Roxie. Although she lives in a suburb, there's no white picket fence or fancy house, just a simple home with a relaxing backyard. Mary is the author of '*Teachable Moments: An Insider's Guide to Pregnancy, Drinking, Drugs, Suicide, Testing, Lunch and Other Life Issues*' published in 2013, which is a book about her work as a school counselor. Steve and Caprice had made appearances in *Teachable Moments*. In addition to writing Mary still enjoys traveling and playing piano, as well as machine embroidery, and gardening. She learned to use the Big Green Egg and still has the quilt. Mary has looked into building and owning a log cabin but is aware that they take a great deal of maintenance, so instead of owning one she plans to rent one in Colorado occasionally which seems like the perfect solution. There is not an actual place called Moosefart, but maybe there should be.